From The Pages of *Overlooked: Being and Finding That Diamond in the Rough*

Working hard is not easy, but when there's a reason behind the hard work, it makes the hard work not only bearable, but meaningful. - **CHAPTER 1**

Being alone is scary, but at some point, every man or woman must have the courage to be alone if they truly want to achieve something meaningful in life. - **CHAPTER 2**

If you've never been alone before, when it comes to time step up alone to achieve success, you won't be prepared. - **CHAPTER 2**

The most successful of people off tiny and early successes, thinking of them as stairs. Stairs make you elevate; they make you get off your feet. So, too, do these tiny and early successes. - **CHAPTER 2**

Believe it or not, we'll all been here countless times in our own lives. An opportunity arises seemingly out of nowhere. Do you take advantage of it or let it pass by? - **CHAPTER 3**

Romantic relationships are built on trust. With it, they can be long and enduring. Without it, they will soon wither away. **–CHAPTER 4**

When things aren't going well in life, you've got to think about that one decision that will help you get on track toward your goal. Just know that whatever trouble you are going through, if you can switch the momentum around and see just a speck of light at the end of the tunnel, you can start to not only walk again, but run. - **CHAPTER 4**

Are the most successful born with more innate talent than others? Yes and no. To get in a position of having success, you have to be born with some amount of talent and get lucky to an extent, but the harder you work and smarter and wiser choices you make, the less than luck or being born with talent in the first-place matters. We all run into good luck from time to time in our lives, but the key thing to remember is that if you prepare on the front end, that luck can catapult you forward in ways you would never have dreamed of. People receive good luck all of the time, but for the most part, they aren't prepared to take advantage of it. - **CHAPTER 5**

Often times, we think of discouragement as a negative for a young-ster in their quest for success, but we should all know that it can fuel the flame for someone to succeed much more than an encouraging word can. This it is produces a sense of urgency in that person that be thwarted because it so personal. Hearing you can't do this or that can produce the grit that Duckworth claims is needed in her book: extreme motivation. - **CHAPTER 5**

So, be brave when you are under pressure, but when there is no pressure at all, you must take that opportunity to be bold. **– CHAP-TER 6**

When you get stung with discouragement, don't try to push it away; let it stick around for a while to give you the motivation to not only get going, but get to the top. - **CHAPTER 6**

"When people's eyebrows are raised around you, they are clearly surprised. For the most part in people's lives, they rarely see any-thing out of the ordinary, so when they do, you can be sure they will react. On the front end, you have to put the ridiculous measure in place to get that ridiculous result, thus tranforming you from being overlooked to becoming out of the ordinary. - **CHAPTER 7**

What's more impressive? Several hundred mediocre people thinking you'll be a success or a few stand-outs thinking you would be a success. For me, I'll take the latter *every single* time. Here's why: people that I have been successful themselves know first-hand what it takes to have success, while those several hundred mediocre people are only guessing. - **CHAPTER 7**

"To be a friend, you have to be four things to that other person: encouraging, consistent, loyal and willing to sacrifice for that person." - **CHAPTER 7**

Coasting after success is not only normal, it's natural. Once you've reached the top of the mountain, there is no more climbing to be done. But for more the most successful, there are always more mountains to climb, always more races to run, always more treasure to be found. - **CHAPTER 9**

"That's how you succeed in life: while most people are celebrating when they win, you need to be focused on your next mission, plotting strategy about how you can be better the next time." - **CHAPTER 9**

"We can count on God helping us to his steer the ship, but even with Him helping you set sail, you still need to be the captain." - **CHAPTER 10**

"When you're initially overlooked, you and others around you often times draw up the conclusion that you are not good enough. When that happens to you, be thankful for it, because discouragement can be a good thing. A flower needs both shade and sun to grow; too much sun can overheat the flower causing it to die." - **CHAPTER 10**

ALSO BY THOMAS FELLOWS

Forget Self-Help
He Spoke with Authority
The Criminal
Mrs. Dubose's Last Wish
Listen Up
Alone at The Lunch Table
When You See It
After the Shampoo
Input-Output

TO BE PUBLISHED IN THE FUTURE BY THOMAS FELLOWS

RELATIVELY SPEAKING: WHEN AND WHEN NOT TO COMPARE YOURSELF TO THE REST

OVERLOOKED: BEING AND FINDING THAT DIAMOND IN THE ROUGH

ROLLING THE DICE: RISK AVERSION EXPLAINED

CONSTANT ENABLING: CREATING AN ATMOSPHERE OF PERMANENT CHANGE

SETTING PROPER EXPEXTATIONS: ALLOWING YOURSELF TO GET CAUGHT OFF GUARD LESS

LOST AND FOUND: BRING OUT THE BOX

REIN HIM IN: BE BOLD, FORGET THE LASSO

CALLED OUT: LEARNING TO CAPITALIZE FROM CRITICISM

BURN THE BRIDGE: YOU DON'T NEED THEM AFTER ALL

NEVER MET A STRANGER: TOPPLING TIMIDITY

THE IMPOSSIBLE SWITCH: PERSONALITIES DON'T TURN ON AND OFF

OVER AND OVER AGAIN: PERFECT PRACTICE MAKES PERFECT

PAPER & PENCIL: CALCULATIONS NOT ONLY ALLOWED BUT ENCOIRAGED

Overlooked

Being and Finding That Diamond in the Rough

Thomas Fellows

Overlooked

Finding and Being That Diamond in the Rough
© 2022 Thomas Fellows

ISBN 978-1-954617-45-2 paperback

978-1-954617-46-9 eBook

www.yawnspublishing.com

678-880-1922
Canton, Georgia

This book is printed exactly as the author intended, without editorial input or reference verification from Yawn's Publishing. For information on bulk purchases, please contact Yawn's Publishing.

Printed in the United States of America

CONTENTS

"It's amazing the way things, apparently disconnected, hang together." – Charlie, *Flowers for Algernon*. Daniel Keyes

"During the break, he visited his father's grave for the first and last time. He never told anyone about what he thought, did, or said there, yet it is not hard to imagine he might have looked down at his father with a mixture of satisfaction and sadness. He could only be proud of how far he had come but must have been sad to remember that his father had never seen greatness in him. It had to be enough that he had proven his father wrong." **– Michael Gerhardt, *Lincoln's Mentors: The Education of a Leader***

In the Brave Ones CNBC Interview with Bill McDermott:
CNBC: Underdog or Over-Achiever?
BM: Underdog, because it keeps you humble, to remember where you came from

"I'm alone and outgunned, scared and inexperienced, but I'm *right*."
– John Grisham, *The Rainmaker*

Introduction

The English language is possibly the most complex language out there. Meanings can change drastically if you slightly alter words in them. For instance, what if a young man sees an attractive female in the bar? Couldn't you presume that she gets looked at over and over again? This, for her, of course is a good thing. But does this mean that getting looked at over and over again is always a good thing? Not necessarily. Consider a CEO possibly buying another company. Say, for instance, she has to look at the deal that her CFO gave to her over and over again. That would change the meaning of the phrase *over and over again* because she is not initially sold on the idea that buying the company would be a good thing. The CFO would prefer that she look at it once and be sold immediately.

This booked is entitled *Overlooked: Finding and Being That Diamond in the Rough.* We've been told throughout our life that being overlooked is a bad thing because it means that people are not interested in you. There is only one problem with this way of thinking, however: it assumes that those people know what they are talking about. Throughout history, we've been reminded that progress depends on challenging the status quo, thinking outside the box, and to come out on top, to quote Wayne Gretsky's father, you've got to "skate to where the puck is going, rather than skating to where the puck is."

What if there was a way to pick a stock like Amazon, predict that Tom Brady would be the best NFL quarterback of all time, or if you're looking to improve yourself, become a late bloomer and have the admiration of the opposite sex and have people of your same sex envy you?

Through my usual use of literature historical figures, scripture, popular music, and popular movies, and my own personal experiences, I try to encourage you, the reader, to not only surprise people with your success, but be surprised less when you find out certain people are successful. Malcom Gladwell once said, "good writing does not succeed or fail on the strength of its ability to persuade. It succeeds or fails on the strength of its ability to engage you, to make you think, to give you a glimpse into someone else's head." I hope I achieved this throughout the pages of *Overlooked*.

1

Just Ain't So

Before the movie even starts, you know *The Big Short* is going to be a movie that highlights the fact that in life, we're always thrown a curve ball; it's the ones who can tell that they're being thrown one though who can knock that pitch out of the park for a homerun rather than simply swinging and missing. Here is the quote below that is shown:

It ain't what you don't know that gets you into trouble
It's what you know for sure that just ain't so. — Mark Twain

I was recently back in my hometown of Atlanta catching up with a friend who was in commercial real estate. Commercial real estate has been booming over the last fifty years in Atlanta and it appeared that no end was in sight for those in the business, but then COVID-19 happened. Companies realized that spending so much money on office space was unneeded because their employees could just be just as productive at home. Additionally, employees could benefit themselves because they wouldn't have to make the commute, which would save them both time and money on gas and car repairs.

One thing to keep in mind, however, is that there are always winners and losers when an unforeseen event occurs. What this book attempts to explain is that although there is definitely luck in the outcome of unforeseen event happening, if you prepare yourself well on the front end, you'll find yourself able to spot those events better. The winner of the fall out from the COVID-19 pandemic was definitely a company I'm sure you're familiar with by now called Zoom Video Communications. In January of 2020, at the start of the pandemic, the stock was trading at 76.3. Just nine months later, it would zoom up (no pun intended) to 470.11. If you had put $10,000 in the stock, it would have been worth $61,598. But to be realistic, who could have foreseen anything like this coming? Nobody.

When we get back to *The Big Short*, we can see how they picked the diamond in the rough by getting less emotional and subjective about numbers and data, and more objective and dismal about them. In the scene after the Mark Twain quote, we're introduced to Jared Vennett, a trader at Morgan Stanley who narrates the whole movie. Almost everybody in life skates to where the puck is, rather to where the puck is going. But with that being said, there are still many in life who think that they are skating to where the puck is going only to find out that there is no action where they have skated to.

Vennett explains that until the late 1970's, banking was an industry with little if any action until the mortgage-backed security came on to the scene. Up until that point, mortgage bankers rarely made a lot of money because the yield always stayed the same. But then Lewis Ranieri, a banker with the Salomon Brothers, concocted a way to put all the mortgages together. What made this more appealing is that while the risk was still small, the yield in the payouts went way up. Ranieri, and the rest of the world for that matter, figured that nothing could ever go wrong because people always paid their mortgage.

What I've realized in life is that the "sure thing" isn't always the "sure thing." We often have a false sense of why things happen. Malcom Gladwell writes about this at length in his book *Outliers: The Story of Success*. One of the ways he explains just this is the success that Bill Gates has had. When you think of Bill Gates, you think of someone who can outthink and out work anybody, but when Gladwell explains the rise of Gates, it is plain to see that there was a lot of luck involved for Gates to become one of the richest and powerful persons on the planet.

> Opportunity number one was that Gates got sent to Lakeside[1]. How many high-schools in the world had access to a time-sharing terminal in 1968? Opportunity number two was that the mothers of Lakeside had enough money to pay for the school's computer fees. Number three was that, when that money ran out, one of the parents happened to work at C-Cubed, which happened to need someone to check its code on the weekends, and which also happened not to care if weekends turned into weeknights. Number four was that Gates just happened to find out about ISI, and ISI just happened to need someone to work on its payroll software. Number five was that Gates happened to live within walking distance of the University of Washington.

---

[1] Lakeside was the elite private school that Gates attended. Lakeside's average ACT/SAT is in the 97th and 96th percentile and its graduates regularly go on to attend Harvard, Yale, Washington, Columbia, Brown and Stanford among others.

Number six was that the university happened to have free computer time between three and six in the morning. Number seven was that TRW happened to call Bud Pembroke[2]. Number eight was that the best programmers Pembroke knew for that particular problem happened to be two high school kids. And number nine was that Lakeside was willing to let those kids spend their spring term miles away, writing code.

Just as Gates got lucky, I, too, also got very lucky in the success that I have been having in terms of writing. First, let's talk about the level of education I have received from K-12. Out of all the private high-schools, Westminster ranks in the top 1/700th percentile. I learned how to use academic databases such as JSTOR sophomore year when most people, even people who end up going to college, don't know how to use one. My history teacher didn't teach us using textbooks, but instead taught us how to use primary sources, which typically is only taught and introduced to history majors in college. Then there's the fact that my father is one of the most well-known trial attorneys in the nation and that our primary method of communication during the last nine years has been email. He graduated from Bucknell in three years and would go on to Georgetown Law School, where he would be editor of the Law Review there. Then there's the fact that I have bipolar disorder, which many great writers have. As Gladwell states in *Outliers,* "who we are cannot be separated from where we're from.[3]"

---

[2] Pembroke was the founder of a technology company that had coincidentally just signed a contract in southern Washington state.
[3] We'll go into the 10,000 hours rule you've probably heard of later in the book and how that theory has proven true in my success.

We follow three groups of people throughout the movie who have the insight to bet against the housing market, something that no one thought would happen, not even the media. One character we're introduced to early on in Mark Baum. Venner, still narrating, when introducing him, says, "Mark Baum had built his career on never assuming anyone or any company was legit without proving it. When he was a kid, he excelled at studying the Talmud in Yeshiva. Whatever, but one days his Rabbi told his mom why:"

Rabbi: Paul is a fine boy and Mark is an excellent student of the Toran and Talmud.
Mark's mother: Then what's the problem, Rabbi?
Rabbi: It's the reason Mark is studying so hard. He's looking for inconstancies in the word of God.
Mark's mother: So, has he found any?

Venner goes on to narrate that, "later, Baum started his own fund on Wallstreet. He had an amazing nose for bull crap, and he wasn't afraid to let anyone know when and where the bull had gone number two."

I was the exact same way growing up. Ironically, Malcom Gladwell also talks about this in *Outliers*, but we'll get to this later on. Most kids when they are seven and eight are listening to whatever any adults say and never questions them: not me, however. My best friend in the neighborhood loves to tell the story of me doubting the throwing ability of another's friend father, and in first grade, when we had career week and a father went on gushing and gushing about how much he loved his job, I had the thought to ask him if he would do it for free. Not to be outdone, in second grade, when

I was having speech therapy lessons, I can remember when they therapist said she was doing it to help me, I claimed she was doing it to make money. Flash forward twenty-five years, and I have been still keen to see what people's ulterior motives are. Here's a back-and-forth email between Michael Gerhardt and I where I comment on the fine job he did on keeping his own opinion of Lincoln from getting in the way of writing about him in his book, *Lincoln's Mentors*.

gerhardt <gerhardt@email.unc.edu>
Tue 3/22/2022 12:00 PM
To:
  • Thomas Fellows
Thanks!
Thomas Fellows
Tue 3/22/2022 11:51 AM
To:
  • gerhardt <gerhardt@email.unc.edu>
Very creative ending, not describing the assassination, and

good job of straying away from off the cuff comments about Lincoln that encourage readers to think positively or negatively of Lincoln...

Robert E. Lee: A Biography: Thomas, Emory M.: 9780393316315: Amazon.com: Books

Reading the Man: A Portrait of Robert E. Lee Through His Private Letters: Pryor, Elizabeth Brown: 9780143113904: Amazon.com: Books

Both of these books on Lee fail to do that.

In the first book, Thomas talks about a slave dying who was with Lee in Savannah, and suggests that he was really sad to convince readers that he cared more about slaves than he really did and in Pryor's book she makes a comment that Lee liked to be around women and animals because he could control them unlike men...

Thomas Fellows
thomas@thfellows.com
thfellows.com

Somehow Atticus had hit her hard in a way that was not clear with me, but it gave him no pleasure to do so. **- Scout, To Kill a Mockingbird** by Harper Lee

Nassir Ghaemi talks about this in *A First-Rate Madness: Uncovering the Link Between Mental Illness and Leadership.* This is what he says:

Some people are neither depressed nor manic, but they aren't mentally healthy either. They have *abnormal personalities or temperaments.* Personality or temperament is just as biological as mental illness, though most of us think otherwise. Our basic temperaments are set by the time we reach kindergarten; studies show that those basic temperaments measured at age three persist and predict adult personality at age eighteen. From then onward as well, despite what many intuitively believe, our basic personality traits change little throughout adulthood and into old age. We may get wiser as we get older, but we do not become less introverted, or more open to experience, or less neurotic (to mention three basic personality traits).

Someone who was open to experience from an early age was Bill McDermott, current CEO of ServiceNow[4], and past CEO of SAP. I met McDermott off a cold email seven years ago and himself, along with his right-hand man, Nick Tzitzon, have provided encouragement and advice that has put me in the position to have the success I am having today. Although I am probably the last person to be dispensing advice on parenting considering I not only have kids of my own, don't have a wife, and haven't even dated anyone in the past ten years, it might be worth the time to at least hear me out because of the number of psychology books and biographies I have read in the last few years. Additionally, I have been around many successful people *and* unsuccessful people[5].

Anyway, when we get back to McDermott, we see that he was not afraid to take risks and be bold, even from an early age. Here's an excerpt from his memoir, *Winners Dream: A Journey from Corner Office to Corner Store*

---

[4] You've possibly heard of SAP, but probably not ServiceNow. Because McDermott hit certain thresholds in his second full year at ServiceNow, he was paid an astonishing $165 million (about 98% in stock) in 2021, making him the third highest paid CEO in the country. He was awarded the stock because he doubled the company in just his second year of being there. If he hadn't of done that, he wouldn't had received a dime of the bonus.

[5] You can learn from both, right? Do what the successful people are doing, and you'll become successful, and do the opposite of what the unsuccessful people are doing, and you'll become successful.

Whenever I had to make a big decision, my mother would tell me that as long as I could put my name and photo next to my actions if they appeared on the front page of the *New York Times*, I shouldn't hesitate to go for what I wanted. I felt guilty about quitting my jobs at Finast and Amato's, but I knew the deli was a much better deal for me than balancing multiple jobs, and not just because of the money. I wanted one purpose to pour myself into versus multiple missions. Just looking around that deli, I sensed a mission.

The first thing I had to learn about was the meat slicer, so that I could make sandwiches. The machine was easy enough to use, as long as I didn't rush. I lost a few fingertips, but they grow back as long as you don't slice the bone. I also learned how to run the register, stock the deli's shelves, and fill the refrigerator when suppliers delivered new shipments. Staples like potato and egg salad arrived in big plastic buckets a few times a week.

I worked hard, as slacking off was not part of my genetic code, but I didn't aspire to be the deli manager or anything.

After about a year, Bob wanted out. He coleased the deli and the adjacent Sunoco gas station with his business partner: a man named Eddie, who drove an Eldorado convertible. Once, Eddie took me to the "21" Club in Manhattan. I remember wearing my only suit and tie. When we entered the dark nook of the historic restaurant, everyone we saw seemed to know him. I was next to a man who could handle himself, and it made an impression on me. I wanted to be just like Eddie—but when Bob wanted to sell, so did he.

The deli and the gas station were not easy businesses to unload. Sunoco's parent company, Sunmark Industries, owned the land under both the station and the store. Bob and Eddie only leased the land and the right to operate each facility on a year-to-year basis. Any new owner was buying only those rights, knowing that

Sunmark could take back the lease, or repurpose the land, after any twelve-month period—which left whoever owned the lease little if any security. Eventually a local entrepreneur named Ernie stepped up and offered Bob and Eddie $50,000, cash. They accepted. But Ernie was interested only in the gas station. For him, the convenience store was just an inconvenience, so he kept me on to oversee operations. I got to keep my job and take on more responsibility.

This was the first time I was in charge of a business, and I loved being able to think of an idea and, *pow*, make it happen. I spruced up the place a bit, made a few changes, and our business started to improve. As I balanced high school and work, I began to feel as if I was coming into my own—until summer.

Before I left town for my family's annual vacation to the Jersey Shore, Ernie panicked. He needed someone to man the deli while I was gone, so he placed an ad in the newspaper for short-term help, but the guy he hired robbed us. He and some buddies came to the deli one night and stole almost everything. All the stock, the equipment. Even the slicer. The place was wiped out. When I returned from vacation, the cinderblock building looked like a bomb shelter. I was upset when I saw what had happened. Even before Ernie put me in charge of the deli, I'd invested a lot of time and effort into working there, making it better, and I had come to feel a sense of ownership. Worse, with nothing to sell, we had no customers, so I was out of a job.

Ernie's solution was to try to unload the deli's lease for half of what he originally paid, but people thought it was overpriced because the real value was in the gas station, and nobody wanted to risk $25,000 to lease a shell from a big corporation that could cut him loose on a whim. The building sat idle into the fall, until Ernie caved.

It wasn't as if I hadn't thought about buying it. In theory, it made no sense: I didn't have the money. I was in high school full-time. But embedded in my upbringing was a philosophy I was about to test: never let the circumstances of a moment supersede the size of your dreams. Rules, assumptions, and doubts were no match for my will, creativity, and hard work. If I wanted something, I would find a way.

I did the math, figuring out how much I could make every month after paying for products and employees. When I talked to my parents about buying the deli, they didn't think I was crazy. They trusted me, they knew I was driven, and they thought I was smart, so they believed that, yes, I would find a way to make it work. And because they believed in me, I believed in myself even more. Plus, they offered to help. Mom said she would oversee the deli when I was at school, and my father, brother, and sister would also pitch in.

So when Ernie asked me to have dinner with him at Amato's, I'd done my homework. Sitting across from him in one of the dark leather booths, being served by a waiter in a tux like I used to wear, I listened to Ernie tell me I could have the deli for $12,500. We both knew I didn't have that kind of cash, but with my plan and my family's support, I had the confidence of someone twice my age, and with much more experience.

"Ernie, it's not going to happen, but"—I had my pitch ready—"give me a fifty-five-hundred-dollar loan, and make it seven thousand with interest, with payments due monthly. I'll pay it all off in a year. If I don't pay you back in twelve months, whatever improvements I made, whatever stock I have, whatever I put into the place, it's yours. You get it all." I paused for a second. I was holding myself accountable for my own success. If I failed, I lost. But if I succeeded and paid Ernie back the money on time, I would own everything, including the lease for the deli, and have nothing to lose. He looked at me. I'd presented Ernie with an idea that he hadn't considered. But Ernie was a street-savvy businessman.

"All right, kid, you got a deal." We shook hands in the dimly lit restaurant.

I knew that I was going to do a lot more than just pay Ernie back. I saw a little store without limits and was determined to build that deli into the best place in the neighborhood.

I wanted one purpose to pour myself into versus multiple missions. Just looking around that deli, I sensed a mission - Working hard is not easy, but when there's a reason behind the hard work, it makes the hard work not only bearable, but meaningful. David Brooks says something similar in *The Road to Character* when he says, "For most of us, there is nothing intrinsically noble about suffering. Just as failure is sometimes just failure (and not your path to becoming the next Steve Jobs), suffering is sometimes just destructive, to be exited or medicated as quickly as possible. When it is not connected to some larger purpose beyond itself, suffering shrinks or annihilates people. When it is not understood as a piece of a larger process, it leads to doubt, nihilism, and despair." At the end of the excerpt, McDermott says that "I saw a little store without limits and was determined to build that deli into the best place in the neighborhood." Is there anything in your own life that you are determined to see grow? If you can find that thing, you'll be well on your way to making a difference in the world.

The most important thing that McDermott says in the excerpt is that "embedded in my upbringing was a philosophy I was about to test: never let the circumstances of a moment supersede the size of your dreams. Rules, assumptions, and doubts were no match for my will, creativity, and hard work. If I wanted something, I would find a way." While McDermott[6] clearly has a very strong business acumen, knows technology well and knows how to strategize and lead teams, he'll be the first one to tell you that he doesn't possess the rawest intelligence. That is, he is more of a divergent thinker, rather than a convergent thinker. Convergent thinking is doing a calculus problem, whereas divergent thinking is thinking of how many uses a tin can has. Any Fortune 500 CEO in their right mind values divergent thinking rather than convergent thinking because the former pushes the needle and impacts the bottom line, while the latter leaves a company stagnant.

If anybody needed someone with divergent thinking, creativity, and a strong work ethic, it was God near the beginning of time. Genesis 6:1-8 reads that

"When human beings began to increase in number on the earth and daughters were born to them, the sons of God saw that the daughters of humans were beautiful, and they married any of them they chose. Then the Lord said, "My Spirit will not contend with[a] humans forever, for they are mortal[b]; their days will be a hundred and twenty years."

---

[6] McDermott rose through the ranks at Xerox to become the youngest Division President, as the first American and youngest CEO of SAP, he led SAP from a market cap of $39 billion to $156 billion, and since his tenure at ServiceNow, has brought it from 847 to 470 in the Fortune 1000 Rankings in just 3 years.

The Nephilim were on the earth in those days—and also afterward—when the sons of God went to the daughters of humans and had children by them. They were the heroes of old, men of renown.

The Lord saw how great the wickedness of the human race had become on the earth, and that every inclination of the thoughts of the human heart was only evil all the time. The Lord regretted that he had made human beings on the earth, and his heart was deeply troubled. So the Lord said, "I will wipe from the face of the earth the human race I have created—and with them the animals, the birds and the creatures that move along the ground—for I regret that I have made them." But Noah found favor in the eyes of the Lord. And, for Noah, he might have been very well belting out the lyrics from "Eh Hee" by Dave Matthews Band when he sings,

> *Praise God, who has many names*
> *But the devil has many more*
> *And with the love that my mother gave me*
> *I'm gonna drop the devil to the floor*
> *I'm gonna drop the devil to his knees*
> *I'm gonna drop the devil to his knees*

Dropping the devil to his knees takes not only confidence in yourself, but also extreme confidence in knowing that the Lord will provide what you need to fulfill his mission. Just as I explained in *He Spoke with Authority: Get, Then Give the Advantage of Confidence*, our first reaction when we realize that God wants to use us is pure fear. That is when we must remember the wise words of Marriane Williamson when she says asks, "Who am I to be brilliant, gorgeous, talented, fabulous?' Actually, who are you not to be? You are a child of

God." Anyone who has made their mark on the world has shared this in common: doubt from others. Don't let that stop you. As we will learn in the next chapter, Mark and other two funds refused to listen, and because they were bold like McDermott and Noah, they crushed that curve ball out of the park rather than taking a swing and a miss. That's what happens when you know what is coming.

2

All Alone

To say that I'm simply unique would be like saying Chicago is simply chilly in February. For quite some time now, I've thought that normalcy is overrated. Consider just the other day: I did two things in one hour that for the average person would be considered not only out of the norm, but also something they would not even think was possible.

I'm always losing things. So, when I couldn't find my cell phone in the morning, I ended up sending a Facebook message to my 5th grade social studies and homeroom teacher. Bear in mind that I had not been in her class in over twenty years. She then called my number so I could figure out where my phone is.

Just minutes later, I would then go to the Whole Foods, which is not too far away from where I live. If you were thinking I would get coffee or breakfast there or go there to grocery shop you would be wrong because I went there to put my recycling in their recycling bin[7]. Literally, as I was doing this, an employee went there

---

[7] For the record, I'm a big fan of the environment and recycling, but not a big fan of the Green New Deal. In fact, Greta Thornberg, who I will talk about later would be proud to know that I was incensed that there were not separate recycling bins at the Houston Open.

to put a bottle in the recycling. Trying to helpful as ever, I just took the bottle myself, put it in the bin, and kept on recycling.

*

Why tell you this story and how has it led to the success I'm having today? Well, in *Talking to Strangers* by Malcom Gladwell, he explains about someone who got accused of murder because she was out of the ordinary.

In the book, he tells the story of Amanda Knox who got accused of murder simply because she was different. In a memoir published in 2011, after she was eventually released from an Italian prison, she writes that, "I was the quirky kid who hung out with the sulky manga-readers, the ostracized gay kids, and the theater geeks." Remind you of me?

Because I'm so unique, people think I'm different and sort of nerdy, so I stopped getting invited to parties and social events in 2016. What happened in my life a year later that has forever changed my life and how others view me? I published my first book in 2017. Is there a coincidence between the two? I think not. In an article entitled, "5 Reason Why Nerds Become Highly Successful in Life" by Modi Palmer Ramos, she says this for reason #2.

2. Friends? What Are Those? Without a bunch of friends, parties, and social events to consume time, most nerds have little to no excuse to not succeed.
Nerds are naturally better about sticking to routines and prioritizing how they choose to spend their time compared to social butterflies. This equals success when less distractions are an issue. Party boys and girls might be busy losing valuable brain cells on keg stands

while nerds are brushing up on their studies to ace those college exams come test time.

When I think of all the time I have had to myself to not only read and write, but also just to think, it should come as no surprise that I have been able to produce so much output in the last few years. I've truly been a loner, going to restaurants by myself, bars, and when I would play golf, I rarely did so with friends; it would usually be by myself. And whereas most people from age twenty-eight to age thirty-two in The South are either married or dating someone, I've done neither.

From all of the biographies I've read in the last several years, I've learned that many great leaders such as Frederick Douglas, Martin Luther King Jr., Robert E. Lee, Abraham Lincoln, and George Marshall also spent much of their time alone. For instance, in Michael Fellman's biography of Lee, Fellman explains that he was not one of the boys.

Lee was most certainly not one of the boys. He neither drank nor participated in yarn telling by the campfire at the end of the day, preferring to retire to his tent, write letters, and read his Bible and Marcus Aurelius.

Being alone is scary, but at some point, every man or woman must have the courage to be alone if they truly want to achieve something meaningful in life.

Michael Burry, another investor at Scion Capital in Silicon Valley, certainly knew what it was to be alone at an early age. Early on in the movie, Burry explains that he felt separated from people because he had a glass eye. To prove this is the case, he flashes back to a football game where his glass eye literally comes out while playing. He feels mortified while people are looking on and even the cheerleaders are aghast at what they see.

I have explained this in past books, but people have also judged me for being different or having bipolar disorder through the years. It certainly hurts to be judged for something you cannot control. But as we will find out later on the movie and what I have found out recently in my own life with all of the success I am having, the ones who dare to be different or are different because God made them that way are some of the most successful people.

But if you've never been alone before, when it comes to time step up alone to achieve success, you won't be prepared. For Burry, he was not afraid, even if it meant his boss berating him. But before we get to that scene, let's address what Burry does well in another scene with a Junior Associate he just hired.

Do Your Own Due Diligence

From Darwin to Einstein, to almost anyone who has challenged to the status quo, one thing that they all had in common was their innate ability to do their own due diligence.

Michael Burry: During the 1930's, the housing market collapsed nationwide by roughly 80% and half of all mortgage debt was in default. There were very specific identifiers, extremely recognizable. I mean for instance, one on the hallmarks of mania is the rapid rise of complexity, and the rates of fraud, and did you know, they're going up? Highest fraud rates since the 1930's
Junior Associate: No, I didn't know that.

Michael Burry: Did you think it was strange when the tech bubble burst in 2001 and the housing market is San Jose, the tech capital of the world, went up?

Junior Associate: No, it's housing, housing is always stable, low-risk.

Michael Burry: I want you to get me the top twenty selling mortgage bonds.

Junior Associate: So, you want to know what the top twenty selling mortgage bonds are.

Michael Burry: No, I want to know what mortgage are in each one

Junior Associate: Aren't those bonds made up of thousands and thousands of mortgages?

Michael Burry: Yeah

Junior Associate: Right away, Dr. Burry

Just like Dr. Burry knew that he would have to think outside the box to achieve the results he wanted, in *The Adventures of Tom Sawyer*, by Mark Twain, Tom, the main character knew that if he followed the words of Ted Turner when he said, "confronted with a problem, I've always looked for an unconventional angle and approach. Nothing sneaky, nothing illegal or unethical, just turning the issue on its head and shifting the advantage to our side," he would find success[8].

SATURDAY morning was come, and all the summer world was bright and fresh, and brimming with life. There was a song in every heart; and if the heart was young the music issued at the lips. There was cheer in every face and a spring in every step. The locust—trees

---

[8] Or at least get out of the day's chores!

were in bloom and the fragrance of the blossoms filled the air. Cardiff Hill, beyond the village and above it, was green with vegetation and it lay just far enough away to seem a Delectable Land, dreamy, reposeful, and inviting.

Tom appeared on the sidewalk with a bucket of whitewash and a long–handled brush. He surveyed the fence, and all gladness left him and a deep melancholy settled down upon his spirit. Thirty yards of board fence nine feet high. Life to him seemed hollow, and existence but a burden. Sighing, he dipped his brush and passed it along the topmost plank; repeated the operation; did it again; compared the insignificant whitewashed streak with the far–reaching continent of unwhitewashed fence, and sat down on a tree–box discouraged. Jim came skipping out at the gate with a tin pail, and singing Buffalo Gals. Bringing water from the town pump had always been hateful work in Tom's eyes, before, but now it did not strike him so. He remembered that there was company at the pump. White, mulatto, and negro boys and girls were always there waiting their turns, resting, trading playthings, quarrelling, fighting, skylarking. And he remembered that although the pump was only a hundred and fifty yards off, Jim never got back with a bucket of water under an hour—and even then somebody generally had to go after him. Tom said:

"Say, Jim, I'll fetch the water if you'll whitewash some."

Jim shook his head and said:

"Can't, Mars Tom. Ole missis, she tole me I got to go an' git dis water an' not stop foolin' roun' wid anybody. She say she spec' Mars Tom gwine to ax me to whitewash, an' so she tole me go 'long an' 'tend to my own business—she 'lowed SHE'D 'tend to de whitewashin'."

"Oh, never you mind what she said, Jim. That's the way she always talks. Gimme the bucket—I won't be gone only a a minute. SHE won't ever know."

"Oh, I dasn't, Mars Tom. Ole missis she'd take an' tar de head off'n me. 'Deed she would."

"SHE! She never licks anybody—whacks 'em over the head with her thimble—and who cares for that, I'd like to know. She talks awful, but talk don't hurt—anyways it don't if she don't cry. Jim, I'll give you a marvel. I'll give you a white alley!"

Jim began to waver.

"White alley, Jim! And it's a bully taw."

"My! Dat's a mighty gay marvel, I tell you! But Mars Tom I's powerful 'fraid ole missis—"

"And besides, if you will I'll show you my sore toe."

Jim was only human—this attraction was too much for him. He put down his pail, took the white alley, and bent over the toe with absorbing interest while the bandage was being unwound. In another moment he was flying down the street with his pail and a tingling rear, Tom was whitewashing with vigor, and Aunt Polly was retiring from the field with a slipper in her hand and triumph in her eye.

But Tom's energy did not last. He began to think of the fun he had planned for this day, and his sorrows multiplied. Soon the free boys would come tripping along on all sorts of delicious expeditions, and they would make a world of fun of him for having to work—the very thought of it burnt him like fire. He got out his worldly wealth and examined it—bits of toys, marbles, and trash; enough to buy an exchange of WORK, maybe, but not half enough to buy so much as half an hour of pure freedom. So he returned his straitened means to his pocket, and gave up the idea of trying to buy the boys. At this dark and hopeless moment an inspiration burst upon him! Nothing less than a great, magnificent inspiration.

He took up his brush and went tranquilly to work. Ben Rogers hove in sight presently—the very boy, of all boys, whose ridicule he had been dreading. Ben's gait was the hop–skip–and–jump—proof enough that his heart was light and his anticipations high. He was eating an apple, and giving a long, melodious whoop, at intervals, followed by a deep–toned ding–dong–dong, ding–dong–dong, for he was personating a steamboat. As he drew near, he slackened speed, took the middle of the street, leaned far over to starboard and rounded to ponderously and with laborious pomp and circumstance—for he was personating the Big Missouri, and considered himself to be drawing nine feet of water. He was boat and captain and engine–bells combined, so he had to imagine himself standing on his own hurricane–deck giving the orders and executing them:

"Stop her, sir! Ting–a–ling–ling!" The headway ran almost out, and he drew up slowly toward the sidewalk.

"Ship up to back! Ting–a–ling–ling!" His arms straightened and stiffened down his sides.

"Set her back on the stabboard! Ting–a–ling–ling! Chow! ch–chow–wow! Chow!" His right hand, meantime, describing stately circles—for it was representing a forty–foot wheel.

"Let her go back on the labboard! Ting–a–lingling! Chow–ch–chow–chow!" The left hand began to describe circles.

"Stop the stabboard! Ting–a–ling–ling! Stop the labboard! Come ahead on the stabboard! Stop her! Let your outside turn over slow! Ting–a–ling–ling! Chow–ow–ow! Get out that head–line! LIVELY now! Come—out with your spring–line—what're you about there! Take a turn round that stump with the bight of it! Stand by that stage, now—let her go! Done with the engines, sir! Ting–a–ling–ling! SH'T! S'H'T! SH'T!" (trying the gauge–cocks).

Tom went on whitewashing—paid no attention to the steamboat. Ben stared a moment and then said: "Hi–YI! YOU'RE up a stump, ain't you!"

No answer. Tom surveyed his last touch with the eye of an artist, then he gave his brush another gentle sweep and surveyed the result, as before. Ben ranged up alongside of him. Tom's mouth watered for the apple, but he stuck to his work. Ben said:

"Hello, old chap, you got to work, hey?"

Tom wheeled suddenly and said:

"Why, it's you, Ben! I warn't noticing."

"Say—I'm going in a–swimming, I am. Don't you wish you could? But of course you'd druther WORK—wouldn't you? Course you would!"

Tom contemplated the boy a bit, and said:

"What do you call work?"

"Why, ain't THAT work?"

Tom resumed his whitewashing, and answered carelessly:

"Well, maybe it is, and maybe it ain't. All I know, is, it suits Tom Sawyer."

"Oh come, now, you don't mean to let on that you LIKE it?"

The brush continued to move.

"Like it? Well, I don't see why I oughtn't to like it. Does a boy get a chance to whitewash a fence every day?"

That put the thing in a new light. Ben stopped nibbling his apple. Tom swept his brush daintily back and forth—stepped back to note the effect—added a touch here and there—criticised the effect again—Ben watching every move and getting more and more interested, more and more absorbed. Presently he said:

"Say, Tom, let ME whitewash a little."

Tom considered, was about to consent; but he altered his mind:

"No—no—I reckon it wouldn't hardly do, Ben. You see, Aunt Polly's awful particular about this fence—right here on the street, you know —but if it was the back fence I wouldn't mind and SHE wouldn't. Yes, she's awful particular about this fence; it's got to be done very careful; I reckon there ain't one boy in a thousand, maybe two thousand, that can do it the way it's got to be done."

"No—is that so? Oh come, now—lemme just try. Only just a little—I'd let YOU, if you was me, Tom."

"Ben, I'd like to, honest injun; but Aunt Polly—well, Jim wanted to do it, but she wouldn't let him; Sid wanted to do it, and she wouldn't let Sid. Now don't you see how I'm fixed? If you was to tackle this fence and anything was to happen to it—"

"Oh, shucks, I'll be just as careful. Now lemme try. Say—I'll give you the core of my apple."

"Well, here—No, Ben, now don't. I'm afeard—"

"I'll give you ALL of it!"

Tom gave up the brush with reluctance in his face, but alacrity in his heart. And while the late steamer Big Missouri worked and sweated in the sun, the retired artist sat on a barrel in the shade close by, dangled his legs, munched his apple, and planned the slaughter of more innocents. There was no lack of material; boys happened along every little while; they came to jeer, but remained to whitewash. By the time Ben was fagged out, Tom had traded the next chance to Billy Fisher for a kite, in good repair; and when he played out, Johnny Miller bought in for a dead rat and a string to swing it with—and so on, and so on, hour after hour. And when the middle of the afternoon came, from being a poor poverty–stricken boy in the morning, Tom was literally rolling in wealth. He had besides the things before mentioned, twelve marbles, part of a jews—harp, a piece of blue bottle—glass to look through, a spool cannon, a key that wouldn't unlock anything, a fragment of chalk, a glass stopper of a decanter, a tin soldier, a couple of tadpoles, six fire—crackers, a kitten with only one eye, a brass doorknob, a dog—collar——but no dog——the handle of a knife, four pieces of orange—peel, and a dilapidated old window sash.

He had had a nice, good, idle time all the while——plenty of company ——and the fence had three coats of whitewash on it! If he hadn't run out of whitewash he would have bankrupted every boy in the village.

Tom said to himself that it was not such a hollow world, after all. He had discovered a great law of human action, without knowing it——namely, that in order to make a man or a boy covet a thing, it is only necessary to make the thing difficult to attain. If he had been a great and wise philosopher, like the writer of this book, he would now have comprehended that Work consists of whatever a body is OBLIGED to do, and that Play consists of whatever a body is not obliged to do. And this would help him to understand why constructing artificial flowers or performing on a tread—mill is work, while rolling ten—pins or climbing Mont Blanc is only amusement. There are wealthy gentlemen in England who drive four—horse passenger—coaches twenty or thirty miles on a daily line, in the summer, because the privilege costs them considerable money; but if they were offered wages for the service, that would turn it into work and then they would resign.

The boy mused awhile over the substantial change which had taken place in his worldly circumstances, and then wended toward headquarters to report.

The great law of human action Tom discovered—in order to make a man or a boy covet a thing, it is only necessary to make it difficult to attain—is one of the chief factors that the housing market collapsed in the first place. President George W. Bush had good intentions of making everyone a home buyer for the first time, but as we know, often times, good intentions pave the way to hell. Burry was obsessed with capitalizing on this. Here is the back and forth between him and the owner of the Fund below:

Michael Burry: It's only a matter of time before someone else sees this investment. We have to act now.

Lawrence Fields: And how do you know these bonds are built on subprime crap? Aren't they filled with hundreds of pages of mortgages?

Michael Burry: I read them.

Lawrence Fields: You read them? No one reads them. Only the lawyers who put them together read them.

Michael Burry: I don't think they even know what they made. The whole housing market is propped up on these bad loans. It's a time bomb, and I want to short it.

Lawrence Fields: Through what instrument, Michael? There are no insurance contracts or options for mortgage bonds! The bonds are too stable. No one would buy them.

Michael Burry: I'm going to get a bank to make me one. Then I'm going to buy a ton of them.

If anyone had to act now, it was George Marshall when he first enlisted at Virginia Military Institute. After being hazed to the point of having to go to the hospital by older classmates, Marshall knew he could either snitch on the people who did it to him, or be brave and not rat them out. He decided the latter, which started his ascent on becoming arguably the most respected general since George Washington. Since he kept his mouth shut, he earned the respect of his classmates early one which would lead him to the success he would have at VMI, which would put him in the position to be successful later on his career.

He might not have known it at the time, but by acting the way he did, he greatly increased his opportunity for success because of a phenomenon known as the "Matthew Effect." It was given this name because of the verse in Matthew, which says, "For unto everyone that hath shall be given, and he shall have abundance. But from him that hath not shalt be taken away even that which he hath." In *Outliers*, Malcom Gladwell writes that

> it is those who are successful, in other words, who are most likely to be given the kinds of special opportunities that lead to further success … It's the best students who get the best teaching and most attention. And it's the biggest nine- and ten-year-olds who get the most coaching and practice. Success is the result of what sociologists like to call, accumulative advantage.

Think about the ascent of my writing career. Early on, I knew that I had to get credibility as soon as possible. That's why, even before the 1st edition of *Forget-Self Help: Reexamining the Golden Rule* came out, I tried to get reviews from papers in the South so that people would think more highly of the book. I did that so that the future reviewers would see that the book had already been reviewed, thus having a higher opinion of it. Who knows if that was the reason *The Atlanta Journal-Constitution* decided to cover it, but those reviews certainly didn't hurt?

Next, after I started to get several reviews from the South, I sent them all to Alabama's biggest outlet, *al.com*. They ended up doing a story on it. All of the media coverage I was getting also gave me the opportunity to be in *The Daily Oklahoman* and a review of the book ran in *The St. Paul Pioneer Press,* which was Minnesota's second biggest media outlet. Apparently, things add up over time. The most successful of people off tiny and early successes, thinking of them as stairs. Stairs make you elevate; they make you get off your feet. So, too, do these tiny and early successes.

The story isn't done there, though. All that media coverage allowed me to get a Wikipedia page, which was a true game-changer. Getting a Wikipedia is extremely difficult; you have to have received a lot of media coverage. Getting that Wikipedia page was huge because it helped me get the interview with CBS Birmingham involving the little-known fact I revealed about Robert E. Lee in my second book, *He Spoke with Authority.* I was able to put an op-ed I wrote five years ago on the "Removal of Confederate Statues" Wikipedia page. Who knows what that CBS Birmingham interview could lead to? Perhaps national coverage?

Even before I have gotten the media coverage I got this year, I reached out to Maria Bartiromo of Fox News and Fox Business channel and was would have gone on Mornings with Maria with Bill McDermott had he been able to do the interview. Again, things add up over time. The most successful of people off tiny and early successes, thinking of them as stairs. Stairs make you elevate; they make you get off your feet. So, too, do these tiny and early successes. For Michael Burry, we will see that success can't come soon enough because his boss and others are breathing down his neck for putting their hard-earned money in what seems like at the time is foolish.

3

No Hands

In the end, Lewsi Ranieri's mortgage-backed security mutated into a monstrosity that collapsed the whole economy and none of the experts or leaders or talking heads had a clue it was coming. I'm guessing most of you still don't really know what happened. Yeah, you got a sound bite you repeat so you don't sound dumb. But there were some who saw it coming. While the whole world was having a big old party, a few outsiders and weirdos saw what no one else could. These outsiders saw the giant lie at the heart of the economy and they it by doing something the rest of the suckers never thought to do: they looked. — **Jared Vennet, Narrator**

Finding the diamond in the rough can be challenging because our mind can only handle and direct so many thoughts at once. Take this example in *Thinking Fast and Slow* by Daniel Kahneman.

An individual has been described by a neighbor as follows: "Steve is very shy and withdrawn, invariably helpful but with little interest in people or in the world of reality. A meek and tidy soul, he has a need for order and structure, and a passion for detail." Is Steve more likely to be a librarian or a farmer?

The resemblance of Steve's personality to that of a stereo-typical librarian strikes everyone immediately, but equally relevant statistical considerations are almost always ignored. Did it occur to you that there are more than 20 male farmers for every male librarian in the United States? Because there are so many more farmers, it is almost certain that more "meek and tidy" souls will be found on tractors than at library information desks. However, we found that participants in our experiments ignored the relevant statistical facts and relied exclusively on resemblance. We proposed that they use resemblance as a simplifying heuristic (roughly, a rule of thumb) to make a difficult judgement. The reliance on the heuristic caused predictable biases (systematic errors) in their predictions.

Here's a somewhat similar scenario that has happened from my own life: I got fired from literally seven jobs in a span of five years, so one would think that I wasn't very good at my job. That couldn't be further from the truth, however. This calendar year I have the potential to make half a million dollars working just 10 to 15 hours a week. In solving problems, we often first assume when we should instead first seek to understand. You can't solve anything without understanding, and assumptions made without understanding become a problem that keeps us from solving them. Before assuming I wasn't talented, we should first ask the question why was I being fired in the first place? For the first three times, it was simply because I ran out of people to call. When you call in a niche industry, this is quite possible despite what people may tell you.

I only lasted one week at one job. One's first assumption is to think this happened because I was that bad, but the fact of the matter is that this happened because I was so talented and could produce. Again, you're probably thinking to yourself don't you want produce in a sales job? The answer is yes, you do. But, if your hiring manager never interviewed you, and feels threatened that you might take his job, then he'll fire you.

For Steve Baum's fund, you have to credit him for having the humility to take his team down to a trip to Florida to find out what was really happening in the real estate world. We often fail to appreciate anecdotal evidence. When what is anecdotal becomes commonplace, must take it seriously. You have to be both active and thorough when making a discovery. Later, we'll see that Baum was even willing to visit a strip club to find as much information as he could.

First, however, two members of his team decide to visit a house where they know that the mortgage hasn't been paid. When they enter it, a father and his son come to the door. One of the members explains to him that his landlord had not been paying the rent. The man turns immediately turns into despair, and explains to him that he had just gotten his son settled in school.

Later, the members of the team join Steve and a few realtors and look at houses in the community. Here is the back and forth between the agent and Mark...

Female Real Estate Agent: The market's in an itsy-bitsy little gully right now. Like everybody said, that's a little bit crazy, let's all just calm down. I sold that house for 350 the year it was built. Two years later, 480, then 585 maybe eighteen months ago. This couple bought it for 650 last year. They'd let it go for that. It would break his heart, but he'd let it go.

Steve: Why is he selling?

Female Real Estate Agent Neither one is working right now.

Male Real Estate Agent: Marlene, you'd say they're motivated, right?

Female Real Estate Agent: As motivated as one can be in this neighborhood. This house on the left, I'd say they're probably motivated.

View on the screen is many houses with For Sale signs in front of them

Mark: Wow, lot of people seem very motivated

Female Real Estate Agent: Oh, it's just this gully, that's all, just nerves. So where do we stand?

Mark: I need to talk to my wife.

Male Real Estate Agent: This market won't last

Mark: Actually, could I talk to a mortgage broker, anybody you recommend, anyone you like?

From the exchange between Mark and the real estate agents, you can tell that they paid heed to my advice above when I said, "when what is anecdotal becomes commonplace, must take it seriously." This is the precise reason why God trusted Noah to carry out his mission. In a sermon preached by CH Spurgeon in 1890, he talks about Noah's everyday habits pleased The Lord greatly, enabling The Lord to have confidence in him:

Notice, first, that *Noah believed in God in his ordinary life.* Before the great test came, before he heard the oracle from the secret place, Noah believed in God. We know that he did, for we read that he walked with God, and in his common conduct he is described as being "a just man, and perfect in his generations." To be just in the sight of God is never possible apart from faith; for "the just shall live by faith." It is a great thing to have faith in the presence of a terrible trial; but the first essential is to have faith for ordinary every-day consumption. Hast thou faith in God as to thy daily bread? Hast thou faith as to thy children and thy house? Hast thou faith about thy trade and business? Hast thou faith in the God of providence?-faith in the God who answers prayer? Is it habitual with thee to roll thy burden upon the Lord? If it be not so with thee, what wilt thou do when the floods break forth? Faith will not come to thee all of a sudden, in the dark night, if thou hast shut it out through all the bright days. Faith must be a constant tenant, not an occasional guest.

Consistency, as Noah was, is essential not only in one's walk with God, but also when accessing making a bold a risk, such as shorting a market that has been stable the last several decades. When we get back to *The Big Short*, we'll see that because the fund was able to see that the mortgage brokers were failing to check the necessary criteria that to see if the future home owners could afford a mortgage, the fund was able to see that there was in fact a bubble. Here are the conversations between the fund and the overly confident mortgage brokers:

Mortgage Broker: So, is Morgan Stanley recruiting us? Is that...
Porter Collins: Oh, no. No. The bank owns our hedge fund but we're not really a part of it. We invest in financial service companies and we're trying to understand the residential mortgage business.

Mark Baum: How many loans do you write each month?

Mortgage Broker: Pffft! About sixty.

Mark Baum: What was it four years ago?

Mortgage Broker: Ten... maybe fifteen.

Mortgage Broker: Yeah, I was a bartender. Now I own a boat.

Danny Moses: You own a boat? So how many of these are, uh, adjustable rate mortgages?

Mortgage Broker: Well, most. Yeah, I'd say about ninety percent. The bonuses on those skyrocketed a few years ago. Adjustables are our bread and honey.

Danny Moses: So do applicants ever get rejected?

Mortgage Broker: [*laughs*] Seriously? Look, if they get rejected, I suck at my job.

Danny Moses: Even if they have no money?

Mortgage Broker: Well, my firm offers NINJA loans - no income, no job. I just leave the income section blank if I want. Corporate doesn't care. These people just want homes, you know, and they just go with the flow.

Danny Moses: Good for you.

Mark Baum: Your companies don't verify?

Mortgage Broker: If I write a loan on Friday afternoon, big bank will buy it by Monday lunch.

Believe it or not, we'll all been here countless times in our own lives. An opportunity arises seemingly out of nowhere. Do you take advantage of it or let it pass by? After observing people in the past few years, I believe I can rightly make the claim that most people are indecisive, pitter-patter, and let the opportunity pass. There have been quite a few times when I have done this myself. The most notable time this happened to me was in the summer of

2016 when I could have moved to Austin to work for Oracle.[9] I made the mistake of running it by my brother and took his advice that the move would be too much for me. Instead of taking that job, where I most likely moved up the ranks rather quickly in the first few years, I listened to him, which honestly wasn't very strategic at all. His reasoning was that I needed to have family close by because I was on so many medications and that it would be a hassle to rent out my condo. Both of those assertions were dead wrong. My mental health was in the fact the best when I was away from my family in Birmingham and Mentone, AL and did use them as a crutch. In terms of the rental market, in 2016 the rental market was not only red hot, but the ease of having someone rent out your condo would have been easy. When you need to be decisive, there are three things you must do: listen and gather information, analyze with keen precision, and act with unthinking sureness.

If anyone needed to act with decisiveness, it was Abraham Lincoln in the early 1860's. In 1864, Lincoln, when speaking of his steady stance surrounding the new elections said, "some single mind must be master, else there will be no agreement in anything." For Lincoln throughout his presidency, projecting strength was always of the utmost importance to him. Anyone who has ever managed or led knows that without this, way their organization, team, or business will never thrive.

Lincoln did what was seen as very controversial then and what some still today see as controversial: he did things that were technically unconstitutional. Here's what he had to say in a letter to Albert Hodges in 1864:

---

[9] Oracle rivals SAP as one of biggest business software companies in the world. It is in the Fortune 100.

My oath ... imposed upon me the duty of preserving, by every indispensable means, that government – that nation – of which the Constitution was the organic law. Was it possible to lose the nation, and yet preserve the Constitution? By general law life *and* limb must be protected; yet often a limb must be amputated to save a life; but a life is never wisely given to save a limb, I felt that measures, otherwise unconstitutional, might become lawful, by becoming indispensable to the preservation of the Constitution, through the preservation of the nation.

In *Lincoln on Leadership* by Donald Phillips, he writes that,

If this passage, written by Lincoln to Albert Hodges in April 1864, were to be read by someone who did not have a general concept of his broad assumption of authority and power, the question might arise: "What did Lincoln *do?*' A better question might be, however, "What did Lincoln *not* do?' In truth, he was so decisive that he left virtually no stone unturned. He took advantage of nearly every situation at hand. Confusion, desperation, and urgency all combined to give Lincoln the perfect opportunity to act. The nation needed a leader's strong hand, and Lincoln provided it.

Look at when Phillips says, "confusion, desperation, and urgency." Didn't all of these things with people when the financial collapse happened in 2008? The answer would be yes for most people except for people like Michael Burry and his team. Instead of having those negative emotions, they were making millions upon millions of dollars. After the mortgage brokers opened up about how things worked, Mark had a little pow-pow with his team.   In doing so, he lived out the first part of my advice I gave earlier of listening and gathering information.

Mark: I don't get it; why are they confessing?
Danny Moses: They're not confessing.
Porter Collins: They're bragging.
They then go back to the mortgage brokers to speak with them…
Mark: Do people have any idea what they are buying?
One mortgage broker shakes his head
Mortgage broker: *laughs first, then says,* I focus on immigrants, you know, once they find out they're getting homeless, they'll sign wherever you tell them to sign, don't ask questions, don't understand the rates.
Mark: And you target immigrants too?
Mortgage broker: Their credit actually isn't bad enough for him.
Mortgage broker: I am a yield guy. I make two thousand on a fixed rate prime, I make two thousand on a fixed rate prime a sub-prime adjustable trust me, I'm not driving that 7-series without strippers no-one on the pole has good credit and they're all cash-rich.
Porter Collins: I think I've heard Warren Buffet say something like this
Mortgage broker: Who is Warren Buffet?
Mark: Okay, strippers, like exotic dancers, right?
Both mortgage brokers: Yeah
Mark: Can you introduce us?
Mortgage broker: Yeah! Yeah!

Since this is a Christian book, we're not going to analyze the stripper scene, but the only reason Mark went to the strip club was again to gather more information; again, in doing so, he lived out my first piece of advice when it comes to being decisive, which is to listen and gather information. After receiving further information and analyzing it, Mark had to do one more thing: act on it with unthinking sureness. Here's the conversation between Mark and his trader after his trip to the strip club to prove he did this.

Mark: Hey, there's a bubble!
Trader: How do you know?
Mark: Trust me. Call vennett buy 50 million in swabs on the nbs Garibaldi's are triple b!
Trader: Mark, are you sure?
Mark: Yeah, yeah! It's time to call bullcrap!
Trader: Bullcrap on what?
Mark: Every freaking thing.

We've all been there before: we've gathered information, we've analyzed it, but we have don't have the guts or courage to act. Mark did, I didn't[10], but what about Tom Sawyer? Does he have the guts and courage to act? We'll find out next chapter...

---

[10] By the way, I totally should have acted. It turns out that Oracle's HQ recently located to Austin, TX. With that level of exposure, I could have been the youngest ever CEO to take over Oracle. Interestingly enough, I had two interviews with Oracle the following year that both stated by cold-emailing VPs. If I hadn't made the mistake of sending a forced and foolish email, I would have been in Austin again, this time already having the exposure of several VPs. I already was planning on breaking the news to Bill McDermott telling I had joined the enemy, which was Oracle. (Larry Ellison, the founder of Oracle and Bill McDermott, have a heated rivalry.) McDermott always takes the high road when they go at it. I once cold-emailed Ellison that I was the Steve Jobs of B2B sales. (Ellison and Steve Jobs were close friends.)

4

Can You Delay?

Romantic relationships are built on trust. With it, they can be long and enduring. Without it, they will soon wither away. Tom Sawyer knew this, which is why he acted in the bold manner he did to woo Becky Thatcher. We're first introduced to Becky Thatcher in Chapter 7. Bold as ever, Tom suggests that they get engaged. Becky agrees, but while they talk out their future plans, accidentally reveals that he had already been engaged before, to an Amy Lawrence.

After that, they play games with one another, each one playing hard to get in hopes that the other will chase. Unfortunately, it doesn't work out and they are both left alone, hoping to be with one another. When things aren't going well in life, you've got to think about that one decision that will help you get on track toward your goal. Just know that whatever trouble you are going through, if you can switch the momentum around and see just a speck of light at the end of the tunnel, you can start to not only walk again, but run. For Tom in Chapter 10, he shows what bold moves can do for someone who went from treading water to surfing a wave. Here is the story of how he won Becky Thatcher below.

THERE was something about Aunt Polly's manner, when she kissed Tom, that swept away his low spirits and made him light-hearted and happy again. He started to school and had the luck of coming upon Becky Thatcher at the head of Meadow Lane. His mood always determined his manner. Without a moment's hesitation he ran to her and said:

"I acted mighty mean to-day, Becky, and I'm so sorry. I won't ever, ever do that way again, as long as ever I live -- please make up, won't you?"

The girl stopped and looked him scornfully in the face:

"I'll thank you to keep yourself TO yourself, Mr. Thomas Sawyer. I'll never speak to you again."

She tossed her head and passed on. Tom was so stunned that he had not even presence of mind enough to say "Who cares, Miss Smarty?" until the right time to say it had gone by. So he said nothing. But he was in a fine rage, nevertheless. He moped into the schoolyard wishing she were a boy, and imagining how he would trounce her if she were. He presently encountered her and delivered a stinging remark as he passed. She hurled one in return, and the angry breach was complete. It seemed to Becky, in her hot resentment, that she could hardly wait for school to "take in," she was so impatient to see Tom flogged for the injured spelling-book. If she had had any linger- ing notion of exposing Alfred Temple, Tom's offensive fling had driven it entirely away.

Poor girl, she did not know how fast she was near- ing trouble herself. The master, Mr. Dobbins, had reached middle age with an unsatisfied ambition. The darling of his desires was, to be a doctor, but poverty had decreed that he should be nothing higher than a village schoolmaster. Every day he took a mysterious book out of his desk and absorbed himself in it at times when no classes were reciting.

He kept that book un- der lock and key. There was not an urchin in school but was perishing to have a glimpse of it, but the chance never came. Every boy and girl had a theory about the nature of that book; but no two theories were alike, and there was no way of getting at the facts in the case. Now, as Becky was passing by the desk, which stood near the door, she noticed that the key was in the lock! It was a precious moment. She glanced around; found herself alone, and the next instant she had the book in her hands. The title-page -- Professor Some- body's ANATOMY -- carried no information to her mind; so she began to turn the leaves. She came at once upon a handsomely engraved and colored frontispiece -- a hu- man figure, stark naked. At that moment a shadow fell on the page and Tom Sawyer stepped in at the door and caught a glimpse of the picture. Becky snatched at the book to close it, and had the hard luck to tear the pictured page half down the middle. She thrust the volume into the desk, turned the key, and burst out crying with shame and vexation.

"Tom Sawyer, you are just as mean as you can be, to sneak up on a person and look at what they're looking at."

"How could I know you was looking at anything?"

"You ought to be ashamed of yourself, Tom Sawyer; you know you're going to tell on me, and oh, what shall I do, what shall I do! I'll be whipped, and I never was whipped in school."

Then she stamped her little foot and said:

"BE so mean if you want to! I know something that's going to happen. You just wait and you'll see! Hateful, hateful, hateful!" -- and she flung out of the house with a new explosion of crying.

Tom stood still, rather flustered by this onslaught. Presently he said to himself:

"What a curious kind of a fool a girl is! Never been licked in school! Shucks! What's a licking! That's just like a girl -- they're so thin-skinned and chicken-hearted. Well, of course I ain't going to tell old Dobbins on this little fool, because there's other ways of getting even on her, that ain't so mean; but what of it? Old Dobbins will ask who it was tore his book. Nobody'll answer. Then he'll do just the way he always does -- ask first one and then t'other, and when he comes to the right girl he'll know it, without any telling. Girls' faces always tell on them. They ain't got any backbone. She'll get licked. Well, it's a kind of a tight place for Becky Thatcher, because there ain't any way out of it." Tom conned the thing a moment longer, and then added: "All right, though; she'd like to see me in just such a fix -- let her sweat it out!"

Tom joined the mob of skylarking scholars outside. In a few moments the master arrived and school "took in." Tom did not feel a strong interest in his studies. Every time he stole a glance at the girls' side of the room Becky's face troubled him. Considering all things, he did not want to pity her, and yet it was all he could do to help it. He could get up no exultation that was really worthy the name. Presently the spelling-book discovery was made, and Tom's mind was entirely full of his own matters for a while after that. Becky roused up from her lethargy of distress and showed good interest in the proceedings. She did not expect that Tom could get out of his trouble by denying that he spilt the ink on the book himself; and she was right. The denial only seemed to make the thing worse for Tom. Becky supposed she would be glad of that, and she tried to believe she was glad of it, but she found she was not certain. When the worst came to the worst, she had an impulse to get up and tell on Alfred Temple, but she made an effort and forced herself to keep still -- because, said she to herself, "he'll tell about me tearing the picture sure. I wouldn't say a word, not to save his life!"

Tom took his whipping and went back to his seat not at all broken-hearted, for he thought it was possible that he had unknowingly upset the ink on the spelling- book himself, in some skylarking bout -- he had denied it for form's sake and because it was custom, and had stuck to the denial from principle.

A whole hour drifted by, the master sat nodding in his throne, the air was drowsy with the hum of study. By and by, Mr. Dobbins straightened himself up, yawn- ed, then unlocked his desk, and reached for his book, but seemed undecided whether to take it out or leave it. Most of the pupils glanced up languidly, but there were two among them that watched his movements with in- tent eyes. Mr. Dobbins fingered his book absently for a while, then took it out and settled himself in his chair to read! Tom shot a glance at Becky. He had seen a hunted and helpless rabbit look as she did, with a gun levelled at its head. Instantly he forgot his quarrel with her. Quick -- something must be done! done in a flash, too! But the very imminence of the emergency paralyzed his invention. Good! -- he had an inspiration! He would run and snatch the book, spring through the door and fly. But his resolution shook for one little instant, and the chance was lost -- the master opened the volume. If Tom only had the wasted opportunity back again! Too late. There was no help for Becky now, he said. The next moment the master faced the school. Every eye sank under his gaze. There was that in it which smote even the innocent with fear. There was silence while one might count ten -- the master was gathering his wrath. Then he spoke: "Who tore this book?"

There was not a sound. One could have heard a pin drop. The stillness continued; the master searched face after face for signs of guilt.

"Benjamin Rogers, did you tear this book?"

A denial. Another pause.

"Joseph Harper, did you?"

Another denial. Tom's uneasiness grew more and more intense under the slow torture of these proceedings. The master scanned the ranks of boys -- considered a while, then turned to the girls:

"Amy Lawrence?"

A shake of the head.

"Gracie Miller?"

The same sign.

"Susan Harper, did you do this?"

Another negative. The next girl was Becky Thatcher. Tom was trembling from head to foot with excitement and a sense of the hopelessness of the situation.

"Rebecca Thatcher" [Tom glanced at her face -- it was white with terror] -- "did you tear -- no, look me in the face" [her hands rose in appeal] -- "did you tear this book?"

A thought shot like lightning through Tom's brain. He sprang to his feet and shouted -- "I done it!"

The school stared in perplexity at this incredible folly. Tom stood a moment, to gather his dismembered faculties; and when he stepped forward to go to his punishment the surprise, the gratitude, the adoration that shone upon him out of poor Becky's eyes seemed pay enough for a hundred floggings. Inspired by the splendor of his own act, he took without an outcry the most merciless flaying that even Mr. Dobbins had ever administered; and also received with indifference the added cruelty of a command to remain two hours after school should be dismissed -- for he knew who would wait for him outside till his captivity was done, and not count the tedious time as loss, either.

Tom went to bed that night planning vengeance against Alfred Temple; for with shame and repentance Becky had told him all, not forgetting her own treachery; but even the longing for vengeance had to give way, soon, to pleasanter musings, and he fell asleep at last with Becky's latest words lingering dreamily in his ear --
"Tom, how COULD you be so noble!"

What Noah did was incredibly hard, what he had to do is what anyone has had to do to be successful: they have had to delay gratification. In this chapter of Tom Sawyer, Tom knew taking the punishment for Becky Thatcher would be hard, but he knew it would be worth it in the end. In the book, *Dopamine Nation: Finding Balance in the Age of Indulgence,* by Anna Lembke, she goes on to explain and highlight how you can make dopamine[11] work for you instead of against you. At one point in the book, Lembke says that, "the reason we're all so miserable may be because we're walking so hard to avoid being miserable." This is certainly true and Lembke speaks to this fact later on in the book when discussing how many people—especially today—have the inability to delay gratification. You see, so many people don't achieve their dreams because they're afraid of the hard work it takes to achieve them in the first place. What this leads to ultimately is continued mediocrity, which in some cases, can lead to depression.

Later, Lembke writes that

---

[11] Dopamine is a type of neurotransmitter. Your body makes it, and your nervous system uses it to send messages between nerve cells. That's why it's sometimes called a chemical messenger. Dopamine plays a role in how we feel pleasure. It's a big part of our unique human ability to think and plan. It helps us strive, focus, and find things interesting.

In today's dopamine-rich ecosystem, we've all become primed for immediate gratification. We want to buy something, and the next day it shows up on our doorstep. We want to know something, and the next second the answer appears on our screen. Are we losing the knack of puzzling things out, or being frustrated while we search for the answer, or having to wait for the things we want?

Lembke is definitely right in her assertion. Rarely do millennials every stick around for a job for more than two years, we even have dinners called "easy mac" and we've become so illiterate as a society that we can only read 280 characters at a time. But for the three funds in *The Big Short* working on the riskiest trade of all time, they had no time to philosophize just what has happened in our world. They had been decisive, and now was their time to cash in. If only success came that easy…

Doggedness

Often in life, to achieve true success, you're going to have setbacks even if you are doing everything the right way and the best to your ability. At the job I am at now, I have lost out on many deals in the last two years but have still continued to grind. Francis Darwin, the son of Charles Darwin, said this when speaking of his father, "Doggedness expresses his frame of mind almost better than perseverance. Perseverance seems hardly to express his almost fierce desire to force the truth to reveal itself."

Doggedness is just what Mark's fund needed when they realized that their swaps weren't going down despite the fact that mortgage defaults had risen dramatically. What do you when you face obstacles impeding your progress at every turn despite the fact that you're doing everything the right way? Do you try to do things differently or do you trust the process?

If Mark's fund was losing trust in someone, that person would be Jared Vennet. After members of the fund yell uncontrollably at him for minutes, they finally have some back and forth about what exactly is going on:

Jared: You guys done?
Danny: Yeah. I think so.
Porter: (holding his side) Jesus. I think I pulled a muscle in my back from yelling.
Vinny: Mortgage defaults are way up. Yet you quote us a higher price on the bonds. Tell me why we shouldn't pull out of this trade right now?
Jared: Listen, I told you when we did this deal the ratings agencies, the SEC and the big banks are clueless. So now their foot's on fire and they think their steak is done and you're surprised?
Mark: This isn't stupidity, this is fraud.
Jared: Hey, if you can tell me the difference between stupid and illegal, and I'll have my wife's brother arrested.

At the end of their discussion, Jared suggests they go to Vegas for the Annual Securitization meeting. Again, you can never do enough listening and gathering feedback before your bold decisive move—especially if you are getting ready to invest millions and millions of dollars.

5

How To Value Things

Mark and his fund end up going to the Vegas conference and discover that there is indeed not only stupidity, but downright fraud in the real estate market. They hold on to their short position as long as possible, and a result, make much money. The same goes with Burry who we mention in the 2nd chapter. Near the end of the movie, Burry writes a letter to investors. Here's an excerpt from the letter:

People want an authority on how they value things, but they choose this authority not based on facts or results; they choose this authority based on what seems authoritative or familiar

When people doubt you, their intuition is that you're doing something out of the ordinary, something that with the talent you possess, seems out of reach. What that person is probably unaware of is the amount of effort that you are willing to put it in to achieve your goal and the passion you have about the subject. We spoke of Malcom Gladwell's *Outliers* earlier in the book. Here an excerpt from his second chapter entitled, "The 10,000-Hour Rule."

For almost a generation, psychologists around the world have been engaged in a spirited debate over a question that most of us would consider to have been settled years ago. The question is this: is there such a thing as innate talent? The obvious answer is yes. Not every hockey player born in January ends up playing at the professional level. Only some do—the innately talented ones. Achievement is talent plus preparation. The problem with this view is that the closer psychologists look at the careers of the gifted, the smaller the role innate talent seems to play and the bigger the role preparation seems to play.

Exhibit A in the talent argument is a study done in the early 1990s by the psychologist K. Anders Ericsson and two colleagues at Berlin's elite Academy of Music. With the help of the Academy's professors, they divided the school's violinists into three groups. In the first group were the stars, the students with the potential to become world-class soloists. In the second were those judged to be merely "good." In the third were students who were unlikely to ever play professionally and who intended to be music teachers in the public school system. All of the violinists were then asked the same question: over the course of your entire career, ever since you first picked up the violin, how many hours have you practiced?

Everyone from all three groups started playing at roughly the same age, around five years old. In those first few years, everyone practiced roughly the same amount, about two or three hours a week. But when the students were around the age of eight, real differences started to emerge. The students who would end up the best in their class began to practice more than everyone else: six hours a week by age nine, eight hours a week by age twelve, sixteen hours a week by age fourteen, and up and up, until by the age of twenty they were practicing—that is, purposefully and single-mindedly playing their instruments with the intent to get better—well over thirty hours a week. In fact, by the age of twenty, the elite performers had each totaled ten thousand hours of practice. By contrast, the merely good students had totaled eight thousand hours, and the future music teachers had totaled just over four thousand hours.

Ericsson and his colleagues then compared amateur pianists with professional pianists. The same pattern emerged. The amateurs never practiced more than about three hours a week over the course of their childhood, and by the age of twenty they had totaled two thousand hours of practice. The professionals, on the other hand, steadily increased their practice time every year, until by the age of twenty they, like the violinists, had reached ten thousand hours.

The striking thing about Ericsson's study is that he and his colleagues couldn't find any "naturals," musicians who floated effortlessly to the top while practicing a fraction of the time their peers did. Nor could they find any "grinds," people who worked harder than everyone else, yet just didn't have what it takes to break the top ranks. Their research suggests that once a musician has enough ability to get into a top music school, the thing that distinguishes one performer from another is how hard he or she works. That's it. And what's more, the people at the very top don't work just harder or even much harder than everyone else. They work much, *much* harder.

The idea that excellence at performing a complex task requires a critical minimum level of practice surfaces again and again in studies of expertise. In fact, researchers have settled on what they believe is the magic number for true expertise: ten thousand hours.

"The emerging picture from such studies is that ten thousand hours of practice is required to achieve the level of mastery associated with being a world-class expert—in anything," writes the neurologist Daniel Levitin. "In study after study, of composers, basketball players, fiction writers, ice skaters, concert pianists, chess players, master criminals, and what have you, this number comes up again and again. Of course, this doesn't address why some people get more out of their practice sessions than others do. But no one has yet found a case in which true world-class expertise was accomplished in less time. It seems that it takes the brain this long to assimilate all that it needs to know to achieve true mastery."

This is true even of people we think of as prodigies. Mozart, for example, famously started writing music at six. But, writes the psychologist Michael Howe in his book *Genius Explained,*

by the standards of mature composers, Mozart's early works are not outstanding. The earliest pieces were all probably written down by his father, and perhaps improved in the process. Many of Wolfgang's childhood compositions, such as the first seven of his concertos for piano and orchestra, are largely arrangements of works by other composers. Of those concertos that only contain music original to Mozart, the earliest that is now regarded as a masterwork (No. 9, K. 271) was not composed until he was twenty-one: by that time Mozart had already been composing concertos for ten years.

The music critic Harold Schonberg goes further: Mozart, he argues, actually "developed late," since he didn't produce his greatest work until he had been composing for more than twenty years.

To become a chess grandmaster also seems to take about ten years. (Only the legendary Bobby Fischer got to that elite level in less than that amount of time: it took him nine years.) And what's ten years? Well, it's roughly how long it takes to put in ten thousand hours of hard practice. Ten thousand hours is the magic number of greatness.

Here is the explanation for what was so puzzling about the rosters of the Czech and Canadian national sports teams. There was practically no one on those teams born after September 1, which doesn't seem to make any sense. You'd think that there should be a fair number of Czech hockey or soccer prodigies born late in the year who are *so* talented that they eventually make their way into the top tier as young adults, despite their birth dates.

But to Ericsson and those who argue against the primacy of talent, that isn't surprising at all. That late-born prodigy doesn't get chosen for the all-star team as an eight-year-old because he's too small. So he doesn't get the extra practice. And without that extra practice, he has no chance at hitting ten thousand hours by the time the professional hockey teams start looking for players. And without ten thousand hours under his belt, there is no way he can ever master the skills necessary to play at the top level. Even Mozart— the greatest musical prodigy of all time—couldn't hit his stride until he had his ten thousand hours in. Practice isn't the thing you do once you're good. It's the thing you do that makes you good.

The other interesting thing about that ten thousand hours, of course, is that ten thousand hours is an *enormous* amount of time. It's all but impossible to reach that number all by yourself by the time you're a young adult. You have to have parents who encourage and support you. You can't be poor, because if you have to hold down a part-time job on the side to help make ends meet, there won't be time left in the day to practice enough. In fact, most people can reach that number only if they get into some kind of special program—like a hockey all-star squad—or if they get some kind of extraordinary opportunity that gives them a chance to put in those hours.

Think about the success I am having with my writing career. Granted, I got really lucky with the fact that that I went to an elite top 75 private school[12], had a father who was a prominent attorney in Georgia, and the fact that I have bipolar disorder, which is something that many great writers have. I had all of those things going for me, but one must keep in mind that for someone my age, in high-school, I was probably in the top [13]1/10,000[th] for the amount of reading I've done. Additionally, not to be overlooked is the amount of encouraging I've done throughout my whole life. I've probably written ninety letters of encouragement over the past five years, which is rare considering not only hardly anyone goes out of their way to encourage, but to take the time to write a letter is even more rare. In my 2nd book *He Spoke with Authority,* I speak to the fact that when I was sending out Facebook messages trying to let people know about my first book, I kept seeing quotes and messages of encouragement to people I sent to while I was in college. What must a self-help author be more than anything else? Well-read and encouraging.

But, to be fair, well-read and encouraging authors are still a dime a dozen. How have I been able to get on TV 90 times this past year? I am incredible at selling. How do you get incredible at selling? You practice hard at it. Even from an early age, I was selling. I sold candy canes, flowers, lemonade, bottled water, baseball cards, and lastly, because I was a such a poor student in high-school in college, I learned how to convince teachers to pass me or give me a better grade. I couldn't get a job easily out of college because I

---

[12] Westminster is the only top 75 school in the Deep South and being in the top 75, puts it at 1/700th in the country in terms of private schools.

[13] I not only read all of what was assigned to me, which would put me in the top 1/1000th percentile, but I read extra material.

had a mediocre GPA from a mediocre school. What did I have to do as a result? I had to convince companies to offer me a job without any experience. When I finally did get employed, I worked for no-name companies, in doing so, learned the art of selling, maybe even better than someone like Larry Ellison of Oracle who is worth billions and billions of dollars. Because I did work for no-name companies, I learned how to think on the fly, be creative, and strategically position my product better than someone my age would have learned had they worked at Microsoft, SAP, Oracle, or SalesForce. Oracle is a Fortune 100 company today, but when it was just a start-up, Instead of Ellison naming his first product Oracle 1.0, he named it Oracle 2.0 because he knew people assume it would be better because all of the bugs would be fixed from the first product. I would do something similar several years at a book conference. When I handed out books to literary agents, I wrote in black sharpie *galley* to take my book more seriously because they would associate that with media coverage, something that Christian authors rarely receive. Gladwell later on says in *Outliers* that "Practice isn't the thing you do once you're good. It's the thing you do that makes you good." With all the practice I got in, I was bound to succeed.

Are the most successful born with more innate talent than others? Yes and no. To get in a position of having success, you have to be born with some amount of talent and get lucky to an extent, but the harder you work and smarter and wiser choices you make, the less than luck or being born with talent in the first-place matters. We all run into good luck from time to time in our lives, but the key thing to remember is that if you prepare on the front end, that luck can catapult you forward in ways you would never have dreamed of. People receive good luck all of the time, but for the most part, they aren't prepared to take advantage of it. For me, I definitely got lucky with the fact that I moved out to Texas, which is still a conservative state, where TV stations would not only be receptive, but appreciate my books that were faith based. But that only happened because I leaned on the advice on Nick Tzitzon[14] who told me I had been fired from a job after a week because I had never interviewed on the front end with the person who was to manage me and that person was threatened that I would take away his job because of my talent. Because of that, I decided to stay in hardware sales, which suited me much better than software sales because instead of relying on raw intelligence, it relied more on grit and practical intelligence, which I possess in droves.

When I first got to know Candler Cook, who is one of my best friends today, I soon realized that he had the rare combination of possessing raw intelligence, practical intelligence, and grit. I reached out to Candler three years ago when I saw that he had come out with a book on his own, which outlined in great detail how he walked on the UGA football team despite having been a third string player on our small private school team and weighing just 145 pounds when he graduated high-school. Having hung out with mostly the "cool kids" from our high school, I had known that Candler was in a "bad" and nerdy fraternity there and that he had been working out a lot during college because I someone posted a picture on our Facebook thread of him making fun of him.

The book entitled *From Underdog to Bulldog* would not only make Malcom Gladwell smile, but another writer who happens to be one of the most famous psychologists in the world named

---

[14] Nick Tzitzon served as SVP of Marketing at SAP and is now the Chief Strategy Officer of ServiceNow

Angela Duckworth. She wrote a book called *Grit: The Power of Passion and Perseverance*, which makes the claim that we overvalue talent and undervalue grit. If you ever get the chance to read the book, be sure to read the preface because it sets the stage for the entire book and the stage is a very personal one:

Growing up, I heard the word genius a lot.
It was always my dad who brought it up. He liked to say, apropos of nothing at all, "You know, you're no genius!" This pronouncement might come in the middle of dinner, during a commercial break for The Love Boat, or after he flopped down on the couch with the Wall Street Journal.
I don't remember how I responded. Maybe I pretended not to hear. My dad's thoughts turned frequently to genius, talent, and who had more than whom. He was deeply concerned with how smart he was. He was deeply concerned with how smart his family was.
I wasn't the only problem. My dad didn't think my brother and sister were geniuses, either. By his yardstick, none of us measured up to Einstein. Apparently, this was a great disappointment. Dad worried that this intellectual handicap would limit what we'd eventually achieve in life.
Two years ago, I was fortunate enough to be awarded a MacArthur Fellowship, sometimes called the "genius grant." You don't apply for the MacArthur. You don't ask your friends or colleagues to nominate you. Instead, a secret committee that includes the top people in your field decides you're doing important and creative work. When I received the unexpected call telling me the news, my first reaction was one of gratitude and amazement. Then my thoughts turned to my dad and his offhand diagnoses of my intellectual potential. He wasn't wrong; I didn't win the MacArthur because I'm

leagues smarter than my fellow psychologists. Instead, he had the right answer ("No, she's not")

to the wrong question ("Is she a genius?").

There was about a month between the MacArthur call and its official announcement. Apart from my husband, I wasn't permitted to tell anyone. That gave me time to ponder the irony of the situation. A girl who is told repeatedly that she's no genius ends up winning an award for being one. The award goes to her because she has discovered that what we eventually accomplish may depend more on our passion and perseverance than on our innate talent. She has by then amassed degrees from some pretty tough schools, but in the third grade, she didn't test high enough for the gifted and talented program. Her parents are Chinese immigrants, but she didn't get lectured on the salvation of hard work. Against stereotype, she can't play a note of piano or violin.

The morning the MacArthur was announced, I walked over to my parents' apartment. My mom and dad had already heard the news, and so had several "aunties," who were calling in rapid succession to offer congratulations. Finally, when the phone stopped ringing, my dad turned to me and said, "I'm proud of you."

I had so much to say in response, but instead I just said, "Thanks, Dad."

There was no sense rehashing the past. I knew that, in fact, he *was* proud of me.

Still, part of me wanted to travel back in time to when I was a young girl. I'd tell him what I know now.

I would say, "Dad, you say I'm no genius. I won't argue with that. You know plenty of people who are smarter than I am." I can imagine his head nodding in sober agreement.

"But let me tell you something. I'm going to grow up to love my work as much as you love yours. I won't just have a job; I'll have a calling. I'll challenge myself every day. When I get knocked down, I'll get back up. I may not be the smartest person in the room, but I'll strive to be the grittiest."

And if he was still listening: "In the long run, Dad, grit may matter more than talent."

All these years later, I have the scientific evidence to prove my point. What's more, I know that grit is mutable, not fixed, and I have insights from research about how to grow it.

This book summarizes everything I've learned about grit.

When I finished writing it, I went to visit my dad. Chapter by chapter, over the course of days, I read him every line. He's been battling Parkinson's disease for the last decade or so, and I'm not entirely sure how much he understood. Still, he seemed to be listening intently, and when I was done, he looked at me. After what felt like an eternity, he nodded once. And then he smiled.

Like Duckworth, in a family surrounded by Ivy Leaguers or near Ivy Leaguers, I was always told I wasn't smart enough to do this or that and look at where I am today[15]. It turns out that General George Marshall was in similar position early on. Turn to the next chapter to see how he responded.

---

[15] This is my 10th book, and I'm 32 years old and I am working on the largest scale government education reform since Thomas Jefferson instituted public schooling

6

Stung and Stuck

Give Angela Duckworth credit. She had the calm and wherewithal not to rub it into her father's face when she had all of the academic success she has had. For General George Marshall and myself, we couldn't help but rub it in when we achieved great success despite the fact that we were overlooked. George Marshall was one that detested braggarts and rarely bragged himself, but when started and continued his ascent to become one of the most decorated United States generals or all time, he couldn't help but write a letter to his brothers making him well aware of the success he was having (and mentioning his relationship with a young woman who had rejected his brother previously was going well.)

To get know the story of General George Marshall well, you must first know that his family—including his father and brother—felt like he would be a complete failure. Often times, we think of discouragement as a negative for a youngster in their quest for success, but we should all know that it can fuel the flame for someone to succeed much more than an encouraging word can. This produces a sense of urgency in that person that cannot only not be thwarted because it so personal. Hearing you can't do this or that can produce exactly the grit that Duckworth claims in needed to have the grit necessary in her book: extreme motivation. If any song epitomizes this feeling, it is "Sk8ter Boi" by Avril Lavigne. The song, released in 2002 of her debut Album "Let Go," is about a skater boy who tries to pursue a girl, but fails miserably because she thinks he is way too good for him. Later in the song however, she explains that the girl regrets her decision when the boy becomes famous and in on MTV. When somebody overlooks you, make a pact to yourself, right then and there, that you will be overlooking them in the future. In doing so, your mind will be transformed in a way to overcome all that is necessary to be that diamond in the rough.

If you ever read a good fiction book or watched a movie, the opening scenes will always give a glimpse for what is ahead. The movie *Rudy* does a perfect of job of this. You see a group of kids and teenagers playing football. Immediately, you know which one is Rudy because he hassles his brother about playing a skill position rather the mundane position of offensive-guard. From the get go, you know that this movie is going to be about the battle between the discouragement Rudy will get from his friends and family, and the sheer determination he has in heart, body, and mind to succeed. The director of the movie continues to hammer out this theme in the second and third scene, which consists of Rudy telling his family he is going to play football at Notre Dame[16], and then in the next scene when Rudy recites verbatim a spirited locker room talk from a famous Notre Dame coach to his best friend.

---

[16] The family thought they had he no shot because he was not only a poor student but Notre Dame was for rich kids and they were members of the working class.

Interestingly enough, in my Cook's biography, *From Underdog to Bulldog*, he faced similar scrutiny before making the UGA[17] football team.   In Chapter 2 of the book entitled "The Journey Begins," he speaks to the fact of just how outrageous his dream of making the UGA football team was.

After being accepted into the University of Georgia in December of my senior year, I turned my attention to the bigger goal: playing football. *How does someone try out for a college football team? I wondered. Do I just show up at a coach's office? Is there even such a thing so college football tryouts? How in the world am I going to make this happen?* I didn't know where to start. I tried doing a Google search, but there was no information online—probably intentionally, because coaches don't want random people showing up at practice. I spoke earlier about Candler possessing a great deal of practical intelligence in addition to having a great deal of raw intelligence.[18] Proof of this is that when he went into the football office to ask about the tryouts, when the coach he was trying to talk to mistook him for someone else, he just went right along with it. I must admit that I possess the

---

[17] Bear in mind that UGA at the time was one of the best teams in the nation in literally the hardest conference in the nation.

[18] To prove that Candler is one of the smartest people in the United States, when he took the GMAT, which is the entrance exam for business school, he scored a 790 out of 800. Apparently 260,000 test takers took the exam the year he took it and only 10 made a 790. There were no perfect scores. This means that Candler, who also went to UGA Business School at night, could have gotten a full-ride to an Ivy league school. He told me that he always wanted to be a Bulldog, though. On the back on Candler's book, it says that he is a finance professional. That vastly understates how successful he has been recently. As a 32-year-old, he'll make $625K, which probably puts him in the top 1/500th percentile for his age.

same practical intelligence that Candler does. When I was first cold-calling during my days at N3, I would ask secretaries to talk to the decision maker, and they would explain to me that he hasn't worked for the company in eight years, I would reply as quickly as possible and with a chuckle, "oh, I still had hair back then!" [19]

If anyone knows how to act calm when the stakes are high, it is Bill McDermott, the CEO of ServiceNow who I have mentioned in earlier chapters. In a CNBC special entitled "Brave Ones," he talks about his ability do so:

> I think I'm the most brave under pressure. When everything is moving fast for everybody else, the field slows down for me. I see it in slow motion. I can see past the situation and chaos and the situation of the chaos and how I'm going to get through.

Although McDermott speaks to the fact that he was brave under pressure, just as important as acting brave under those circumstances is acting bold when there is no pressure at all. So, be brave when you are under pressure, but when there is no pressure at all, you must take that opportunity to be bold.

The fourth scene of *Rudy* is of his high-school practicing their last football game. In that practice, the coach explains that their next game will be many of the players last game because the vast majority of them won't be playing college ball. Rudy didn't want to hear it, however. In the next scene, his teacher in high-

---

[19] Our lists that we got to call were often very outdated. Every now and then you would call, and the secretary would solemnly say that that person was deceased.

school tells him something that both Duckworth and Marshall heard often from their families.

The problem with dreamers is that they are normally not doers.

The fifth scene is much of the same. There's a bus that Rudy gets on that is taking students for a tour of the Notre Dame campus. When Rudy tries to get on, the same teacher who told him not to dream told him that some people aren't meant for college. Have you ever had someone told you that you couldn't do something? How did that make you feel? I suggest next time that happens to you, don't feel discouraged but let it give you a jolt of energy to prove them wrong. I also suggest you listen to DMX' "X Gon Give It to Ya" and crank it on full blast. Just remember that even the most successful people in the world have had doubters in their life, even my role-model, Bill McDermott. Here's an excerpt from his book *Winners Dream* recounting how he felt when he was discouraged at a very young age.

When I was in first grade at St. Ignatius elementary school, Sister Jean Agnes, a teacher who never hesitated to smack my fingers with a ruler to punish me for my poor handwriting, walked up to my mom and dad on parents' night. I was standing next to my father when he asked the Sister how I was doing in school.

"Well, Mr. McDermott," she said, all but ignoring my six-year-old ears, "Bill's a good boy and behaves well, but just don't expect too much of him. He'll probably be a mechanic, or maybe a truck driver." My parents had nothing against mechanics or truck drivers, but a few weeks later, they pulled me out of St. Ignatius.

It was too late. I had overheard the bleak forecast, and despite my parents' obvious disagreement with the nun's assessment of me, her words stung, and then they stuck.

Notice how McDermott says that her words stung and then stuck. When you're overlooked, this constantly happens, but could it be beneficial for this to have happened in McDermott's life and for this to happen in your own life from time to time? Even more counterintuitive, in order to be successful, can it be beneficial for this to happen frequently? Yes.

That's exactly what my friend Candler Cook thought when he failed to make the team for the second time. After he got cut again and the coach left him the most demoralizing note of all time, which read that he could *maybe* play at a D3 school because he wasn't strong enough or fast enough to play SEC football, his friend asked him if he was going to throw the note away. Much to his friend's surprise, he said "no, I'm making copies." When you get stung with discouragement, don't try to push it away, let it stick around for a while to give you the motivation to not only get going, but get to the top.

7

Marsha, Marsha, Marsha

He was not the Model Boy of the village. He knew the model boy well though—and loathed him. — **The Adventures of Tom Sawyer by Mark Twain**

We all know the type: the person with it all: good lucks, good health, smarts, social skills, a good job, a good house. Everything seems to go their way. I'm definitely not that guy. Neither was Tom Sawyer or Noah. We'll get to them next chapter, but first let's examine my short comings.

1. I've been suicidal twice.
2. I haven't dated anyone in ten years and I'm thirty-two in the South.
3. I've had two dates in the last few years last fewer than twenty-five minutes.
4. There was a stretch in 2017 when I literally did not make it to a second date and had ten straight first dates.
5. I've never had a relationship make it past a year.

6. From 2015-2020, I was fired from seven jobs.[20]
7. In 2020, I even got fired from my psychiatrist.
8. I could have been on food stamps in 2018 and 2019 after going to seventeen years of private school.
9. I'm on five medications for mental health.
10. I rarely get invited to parties.

Because no one ever looked my way, or if they did, immediately looked away because they were apparently so disgusted with what they saw, I was left to reflect, and, more importantly, I was forced to get better. I admit, sometimes am I a little bit overdramatic about being overlooked? Yes, I am; I admit it, but it's lead to the success I am having today. I honestly seek out people not taking me seriously or not accepting me because it gives me the fuel I need to order to succeed in the long run.

But as much as I've been overlooked, I had people occasionally say I have potential. What's more impressive? Several hundred mediocre people thinking you'll be a success or a few standouts thinking you would be a success. For me, I'll take the latter *every single* time. Here's why: people that have been successful themselves know first-hand what it takes to have success, while those several hundred mediocre people are only guessing. For me, there have been five people specifically who saw me having success from the first few encounters of getting to know me. They are Tiffany Boozer of Westminster, Sharon Jackson of Samford, Bill McDermott of ServiceNow, Miss Sonya of Samford, and Nick Tzitzon of ServiceNow. What makes them so successful?

---

[20] Believe it or not, I actually got fired from a job where I was doing free work for them. That was a tough pill to swallow.

Tiffany Boozer – would still be at King & Spalding, the best law firm in Atlanta, if she didn't decide to go back into teaching in her mid-thirties. With her tenacity and smarts, she would have been made partner by age forty and would be making seven-figures today.

Sharon Jackson – No elite consulting group like Bain, McKinsey, or BCG is ever going to recruit at Samford because it is not considered an elite enough school, but accounting is the most prestigious major at Samford, and graduates of the program can end up making several hundreds of thousands of dollars a years without taking major entrepreneurial risk. She was in charge of this program.

Miss Sonya – possibly the most beloved employee at Samford during my time there. She swipes cards at the front in the cafeteria. Probably made less than ten dollars an hour while I was there, but generated the most smiles of any employee on campus. She would often hold up the line because she would be talking to students.

Bill McDermott – arguably the hottest CEO in the country. Worth nine-figures today and didn't inherit a dime. Appears more on CNBC more than any other CEO

Nick Tzitzon – Inspires confidence for his employees around him and probably makes $5 million a year, which is tough to do in a big company as an executive.

At the end of the day, despite the fact that I had so much failure in the last few years, I still knew I had people who believed in me at the end of the day, which kept me from giving up on achieving what I knew I was capable of. For Rudy, that person was his best friend, Pete. To be a friend to another, you have to be four things to that other person: encouraging, consistent, loyal and willing to sacrifice for that person[21]. Through the first bit of the movie, Pete is that way towards Rudy in every single scene. In a touching scene where Pete gives Rudy a signature Notre Dame jacket for his birthday, Pete tells Mike, "That he was the only one who took him serious." Pete's only response to him was, "you know what my Dad always said? Having dreams is what makes life tolerable." If we look from an objective view at the situation, why did Pete have so much faith in Rudy? He had what Duckworth says leads to her success in her book *Grit*.

> Why were the highly accomplished so dogged in their pursuit? For most, there was no realistic expectation of ever catching up to their ambitions. In their own eyes, they were never good enough. They were the opposite of complacent. And yet, in a very real sense, they were satisfied being unsatisfied. Each was chasing something of unparalleled interest and importance, and it was the chase—as much as the capture—that was gratifying. Even if some of the things they had to do were boring, or frustrating, or even painful, they wouldn't dream of giving up. Their passion was enduring.

I've had success because I'm the same way; I have followed the advice that Bill McDermott gave me the past five years where he told me to focus on the journey instead of the destination. Even

---

[21] Isn't that how God is towards us?

as I am writing right now, all I want to do is to sleep because of a medication I have been on for fourteen years called Seroquel. It is the most sedating drug out there, but I have to continue to keep taking it because it keeps from going into a manic episode because of my bipolar condition. Are you willing to be gritty enough to accept pain to keep from failing?

My friend Candler Cook sure was willing to accept the pain even if it meant eating it until it literally hurt. He knew he had to gain a lot of weight to play SEC football, but also knew that he had to put it on the right way:

NEW EATING SCHEDULE

An important part of my new plain involved shifting to ten meals a day. I knew there was no way I'd make the team at my current size; I had to get bigger. Eight meals had worked for a while; but I had plateaued, so I needed to bump it up. I started this step the day after I got cut in April.

Within a few days, I could tell I couldn't eat that much without getting physically sick. I wasn't a professional eater, and my stomach could only hold so much food. From bodybuilding websites such as Animal Pak, I learned that whole milk was an excellent way to get calories without eating solid food, so I to my nutrition plan—two gallons per day. Animal Pak also provided ideas for keeping meals enjoyable and interesting—like adding Splenda to oatmeal and including shakes with bananas, peanut butter, and protein powder at some meals.

If you make a big play in a football game, the crowd goes crazy. If you make a big lift in the gym, your friends congratulate you and random people might stop to watch. When you eat an incredible amount of food to get bigger, however, nobody else cares. You must be disciplined and completely self-driven. Eating right is the most important part of gaining muscle, and it's also the most overlooked. I knew a lot of people who worked hard in the gym or at practice but never saw results, because doing the right things one hour a day in the weight room doesn't make up for a bad diet and poor choices in the remaining twenty-three hours.

Because I didn't know anyone else who was on this kind of eating plan, I went online for inspiration. I watched videos on the YouTube channel Muscle Prodigy, and one in particular really helped me through the eating regimen. In the video, called "Motivation for Life," Jaret Grossman talks about the importance of every aspect of a training plan, even when you don't get recognition for it:

> You don't set out to build a wall. Instead you say, "I'm going to lay this brick out as perfectly as a brick can be laid." You do that every single day, and soon enough you will have a wall… In order to get to a thousand, you need a thousands ones[22]. Now each one seems insignificant, but you need every one of those to add up to a thousand.

This perfectly summarized my mentality: every day, every workout, and every meal was like a brick I was putting in

---

[22] The most successful of people off tiny and early successes, thinking of them as stairs. Sounds a light like what I said in Chapter 2, right? Stairs make you elevate; they make you get off your feet. So, too, do these tiny and early successes.

place to build a wall. Every brick brought me one small step closer to my goal.

The menu I followed on a typical ten-meal day looked like this:

- 7:15 a.m.: four eggs, (scrambled, fried, or an omelet), two cups of oatmeal, thirty-two ounces of whole milk
- 9:30 a.m.: three egg whites, two sausage patties, two cups of grits, thirty-two ounces of whole milk
- 11:00 a.m.: two ten-ounce steaks, three sweet potatoes, one cup of spinach, thirty-two ounces of whole milk
- 12:30 p.m.: eight ounces of grilled chicken, two cups of white rice, a cup of cantaloupe, three ten-ounce peanut butter and banana smoothies
- 2:00 p.m.: two peanut butter and jelly sandwiches, three sweet potatoes, thirty ounces of whole milk
- 3:30 p.m.: two turkey sandwiches, one banana, thirty-two ounces of whole milk
- 5:30 p.m.: one ten-ounce steak, three sweet potatoes, Caesar salad, three ten-ounce peanut butter and banana smoothies
- 7:00 p.m.: eight ounces of grilled fish (usually tilapia or grouper), two cups of white rice, one cup of watermelon, thirty-two ounces of whole milk
- 10:00 p.m.: four egg whites, one bagel with cream cheese, thirty-two ounces of whole milk

I put this nutrition plan together on my own, based on my class and workout schedule and information I'd read online. In whole milk alone, I consumed about forty-eight hundred calories a day; in total, I was taking in at least fifteen thousand calories. I also drank at least three gallons of water a day. If you're eating that much food, you really need to stay hydrated, especially if you're working out as much as I was.

I had to change my class schedule because of my new eating plan. Starting the fall of my junior year, I scheduled classes so that I never had two in a row. I always had a class, then a break, then a class, and so on. I had to make time to eat before and after every single class.

Now, let's pick out some phrases to dissect how Candler went from being overlooked to eventually making the time and traveling to their bowl games.   Even before that, let's examine the last sentence before that long excerpt.

My ridiculous goals required ridiculous measures

A little bit (or a lot of crazy) can go a long way toward achieving your goals. Vince Lomardi once said time that the only place success comes before hard work is in the dictionary. Even thinking of attempting what Cook did with his new eating schedule would raise some eyebrows, which is exactly what you want to. When people's eyebrows are raised around you, they are clearly surprised. For the most part in people's lives, they rarely see anything out of the ordinary, so when they do, you can be sure they will react. On the front end, you have to put the ridiculous measure in place to get that ridiculous result, thus allowing you from being overlooked to becoming out of the ordinary.

Stevie Williams, when speaking of Tiger Woods, spoke to the fact that one time when they were driving on a highway in Canada, Tiger demanded that Steve stop the car because he thought of a new swing thought that he *had* to practice right then and there. Sound crazy? You have to be that crazy and obsessed if you truly want to reach your goal.

I've never tried to hide the fact that I had tremendous advantages when it came to writing and to my sales career because I come from great wealth. In fact, for the most part, the more and more I read, the more and more I am convinced that coming from great wealth gives you a serious advantage in life, which makes Bill McDermott's success all the more impressive. What I haven't opened up until now is why I have such an impeccable work ethic. Yes, part of the reason comes from going to Westminster, and having siblings and a father who took pride in a strong work ethic, but the fact of the matter is that in some ways I have been blessed to have bipolar disorder. According to a recent article in "Identity in bipolar disorder: Self-worth and achievement" people with bipolar disorder have "inordinately high ambitions" and "may be vulnerable to what has been called contingent self-worth—the idea that one feels worthy of acceptance and self-acceptance only under certain conditions." This is obviously a double-edged sword. On the one hand, it can lead to great success because that person is might try harder to succeed to feel good, but on the other hand it can lead to depression when the person fails.

People with bipolar are willing to work harder for a reward than the average because their reward system is essentially broken. The article goes on further to state that, "greater willingness to expand effort in a pursuit of reward has been found at a behavioral and a physiological level among persons with bipolar in euthymic states and among persons at risk for bipolar disorder. This pattern appears consistent with higher valuation of lower cost of difficult-to-obtain rewards." Writing your 10th book at before your 33rd birthday while at the same time marketing your 4th book and working a full-time job in tech sales could certainly be considered hard to obtain by most people. But for me, it comes rather easily, which in itself seems rather ridiculous as Cook puts it. Apparently, however, I'm in good company because when George Marshall got married for the second time to Katherine Tupper Brown, Marshal's instructors and students hope that it would calm him down a bit and that he would become, "less driven." From my mother, to my mentor Nick Tzitzon as well as others, many have told me to be less driven, less hard on myself. You know why I won't listen to them? I want to keep on working hard so I won't be overlooked, thus wanting to say "Marsha, Marsha, Marsha[23]" all of the time.

---

[23] This is arguably the most famous line in the 1970's sitcom "The Brady Bunch." The line is said by Jan Brady who is constantly being overlooked in her family because her older sister is prettier, more popular, and has a better personality.

8

Could and Couldn't Do

What's the biggest reason why we don't carry out God's will? It might not necessarily be that we are actively trying to disobey him; instead, it might be that we think that we are not capable of serving him because of our checkered past or because we think who am I to do something great for The Lord? When you doubt your own ability to God's great work, you must remember the profound words of Oswald Chambers when he said, "the life of faith is not a life of mounting up with wings, but a life of walking and not fainting…Faith never knows where it is being led, but it loves and knows the One who is leading." When you have blind faith in The Lord, it shows not only reverence for The Lord, but also humility because it shows that your Maker knows best instead of you.

Noah became one of the biggest heroes of the Bible because he lived out the words of Proverbs 3: 5-6 when it says "Trust in the Lord with all your heart and lean not on your own understanding; in all your ways submit to him, and he will make your paths straight." Noah's paths weren't always straight; Genesis tells us that he had a habit of getting drunk from time to time, but that didn't let God stop him from using him to save his creation. God has been using flawed human beings to do His will since the beginning of time. Keeping that in mind, what do you think he has in store for you?

*

Last chapter, we saw that Tom was not the Model Boy, but does that mean that he was overlooked? Not at all. Time and again throughout the book, we see that through his outside of the box thinking, he was able not to become simply the Model Boy, but a hero, and a rich hero at that.   Larry Ellison once said, "when you innovate, be prepared for everyone to call you nuts." You can take that quote a step further, however. Sometimes, in order to lead, you have to be nuts. Early on in George Marshall's career, this proved to be the case. Here's an excerpt from *George Marshall: Defender of the Republic* by David L. Roll that highlights Marshall's willingness to tell authority, even if that authority was the president, that he was wrong.

The president continued around the room, seeking approval from the gathered officials and aides. "Most of them agreed entirely." Marshall recalled, "[and] had very little to say, and were very soothing." When Roosevelt spotted Marshall, whom everyone in the room knew was a candidate to come chief of staff, he said, "Don't you think so, George? In fact, Marshall believed the proposal was amateurish and militarily unsound. Further, he was mildly irritated by Roosevelt's use of his first name, since they barely knew each other. Marshall responded politely, some said coldly: I am sorry, Mr. President, but I don't agree with that at all." Roosevelt gave Marshall a startled look. With that, he adjourned the meeting, a mere half hour after it began. "[W]hen I went out," recalled

Marshall, "they all bade me good-by and said that my tour in Washington was over."

It was a remarkable moment, one that most who were there would never forget. Twenty years earlier Marshall had confronted Black Jack Pershing, the most powerful general in the army, with his version of the truth. Now he had rebuffed the president of the United States. He later explained that he thought FDR's proposal to produce 10,000 planes for $500 million did not take into account the recruitment and training of the pilots, the munitions required, and the infrastructure needed to support a large air armada. Moreover, if Congress was going to appropriate that much money to the army, Marshall and Craig wanted it be used to create more of a balance between ground and air forces. After all, in the fall of 1938, America's regular army of 174,000 ranked eighteenth or nineteenth in the world. Even if Roosevelt had made it clear that he intended to sell most, if not all, of the planes to the British and French, Marshall would probably still have responded negatively because the planes, not to mention increased ground forces, would be needed by the U.S. to deter and defend against an attack on the Western Hemisphere, the possibility of which Roosevelt had just put forth in his argument to the group assembled in the Cabinet Room.

There is no evidence that Marshall had second thoughts about the fact that he was the only one in the packed room to openly disagree with Roosevelt, nor that he believed that he had hurt his chances to be appointed chief of staff. Indeed, he later suggested that the incident in the Cabinet Room may have improved his odds because the president knew that "I would tell him the truth so far as I was personally concerned." Recent Marshall biographers have suggested that he may have deliberately opposed the president in order to get attention. This is sheer speculation—Marshall would not have jeopardized his career by attempting such a ploy.

Considering Marshall was later appointed chief of staff, Roosevelt must have thought Marshall as bold and daring, which is exactly what he needed in his next chief of staff. But for Marshall, he not only had to have those two qualities, he had to know that Roosevelt would possess the humility to listen to his subordinates.

If Rudy needed anyone to listen to him, it was Father Cavanaugh, the priest at Notre Dame. At first, father Cavanaugh thinks that he is seeing him because he wishes to become a priest, but then Rudy tells him his real intention for the meeting. Here is the back and forth between the two:

Father Cavanaugh - Why are you here?
Rudy: I want to go to school at Notre Dame.
Father Cavanaugh: Well, have you applied?
Rudy: No, my grades have never been very good, even though I tried. But I'll try harder. I'll study 20 hours a day if I have to.
Father Cavanaugh: This university, it's not for everybody.
Rudy: Ever since I was a kid, I wanted to go to school here. And ever since I was a kid, everyone said it couldn't be done. My whole life, people have been telling me what I could do and couldn't do. I've always listened to them, believed in what they said. I don't want to do that anymore.
Father Cavanaugh: Okay, Mr. Rudy. Here's the deal...
...Holy Cross Junior College is nearby. I can get you one semester there. You make grades, you get another semester. Maybe with a good GPA...you might have a chance of getting into Notre Dame.

This quote from chapter 4 would be apt to say right about now except for one reason. Can you tell what that reason is?

I suppose it is an unfair question to ask if you haven't seen the movie. The answer is that things were going fairly well for Rudy at that point in his life. He had a good union job, and his beautiful fiancé had just found a house that they could afford and start a family. But that wasn't enough for Rudy; he wanted to achieve his goal of playing football for Notre Dame. Do you remember what Candler Cook said that ridiculous goals require you to have? Ridiculous measures. As Angela Duckworth says in the book, *Grit*: "Our potential is one thing. What we do with it is quite another." Rudy's potential, just like Cook's potential wasn't great to begin with, but in the next chapter we'll examine that talent should be overlooked more often than not, instead of obsessed over.

9

Round Two?

When we look at someone successful, our first thought is to think that that particular person must be someone who has been blessed beyond belief by God. If we take a deeper dive however, it is plain to see that the blessing alone won't produce excellence. According to Dan Chambliss,

> superlative performance is really a confluence of dozens of small skills or activities, each one learned or stumbled upon, which have been carefully drilled into habit and then are fitted together in a synthesized whole. There is nothing extraordinary or superhuman in any of those actions; only the fact that they are done consistently and correctly, and all together, produce excellence.

You could argue the fact that all of my success in my writing career was due to the fact that I came from the upper 1%, but at the same time, there have been millions of people in this country with the same privilege and none have produced or come anywhere close to what I have produced. How have I continued to keep having success while trying to achieve more at the same time? I seemed to have pushed myself beyond limits where people normally don't go. William James, a Harvard psychologist once said that, "the human individual lives usually far within his limits; he possesses powers of various sorts which he habitually fails to use. He energizes below his maximum, and he behaves below his optimum." For most people, this happens because after they have success, they coast. I'm the opposite and the reason why is my bipolar condition. Here's what the same article I mentioned in Chapter 7 says about the mentality I have:

> Beyond extreme cognitive responses to success, people with bipolar disorder appear to also show distinct behavioral responses to small successes. One key study examined the dynamics of goal pursuit in participants with remitted bipolar 1 disorder relative to a control group, in which participants tracked expected and actual progress toward preestablished goals at sequential time points. In general, when participants made more progress on a goal than expected, they decreased efforts toward that goal during the next time point. (Fulford et al., 2010). In other words, they showed a tendency to relax efforts immediately after a small success. Participants with bipolar disorder showed significantly less of this tendency to "coast" following better-than-expected progress toward a goal. These results imply that the same cue that signals the onset of a "rest and reassess" period for most people appears to signal continued persistence for those with bipolar disorder.

Coasting after success is not only normal, it's natural. Once you've reached the top of the mountain, there is no more climbing to be done. But for the most successful, there are always more mountains to climb, always more races to run, always more treasure to be found. If anyone has lived life this way, it is Tiger Woods. In an interview with Steve Williams, his caddie who was on the bag for thirteen of fifteen of Woods' major wins, he quipped that, "One of the most unusual things about working for Tiger, they're were never really any big celebrations, a soon as that tournament was over, the thought was to the next major championship." That's how you succeed in life: while most people are celebrating when they win, you need to be focused on your next mission, plotting strategy about how you can be better the next time.

For Rudy, there wasn't going to be even a first time if he could get his GPA high enough at the community college to enable him to get into Notre Dame. Considering he struggled in highschool, his chances of doing well at Holy Cross seemed unlikely unless he got some help. Often times, what do you need to do in order to get help? Be of help. You see, there was a nerdy TA named D-Bob who had no clue how to get a girl and he proposed that if Rudy helped him find a girl, he would tutor Rudy in exchange for no cost. Again, like I harped on earlier in the book, you have to get some luck to have success.

*

Toughness on one's self and success go hand and hand. Most people are too easy on themselves, but the most successful make it a point be their own worst critic. George Marshall was so successful because he lived life this away. Roll later wrote in his biography that "on twilit winter walks before dinner Katherine had the feeling that her husband "lived outside" of his own body, constantly discipling himself as if he were his own subordinate." Look at yourself that hard and there's no way you'll be overlooked.

Marshall wasn't the only one who looked at himself that way; Cook looked at himself the same way, which is why he got looks, even strange looks. At one point in his biography, Cook tells the reader when he got the strangest look of all. Why did he get it? Wouldn't you stare at someone who was eating a potato in class? I certainly got some stares when I brought my FDR biography into the Houston Open, but I look forward to them staring at me on 60 minutes next year when I am on the show, explaining how I've written 12 books by the time I was 33.

Why I am this ambitious? Again, because of the fact that I have bipolar, I am born with some advantages. According to that article I had mentioned previously, "when most people would tend to experience a sense of satisfaction and contentment in acknowledgment of an acknowledgment, persons with bipolar disorder may already be revving up in preparation toward the next goal[24]." My goal is to create page-turning books, did I achieve my goal? If so, turn the page to the last chapter.

---

[24] While Bill McDermott doesn't have bipolar disorder, his philosophy on celebrating success is the same as mine. In the CNBC interview I mentioned earlier, when asked what advice he would give to his younger self, he told the interviewer that he should have taken more time to celebrate his successes.

10

I Can Keep Up with Them

Rudy ends up doing all he can to get into Notre Dame: he studies, he sacrifices, and he even prays. Still, however, after three semesters, he doesn't get in. With one more semester to go, he decides goes to the church and finds his old friend Father Cavanaugh there. Here is their conversation below:

Father Cavanaugh: Taking your appeal to a higher court.
Rudy: I'm desperate. If I don't get in next semester. If I don't get in next semester. If I don't get in next semester, senior transfers.
Father Cavanaugh: Well, you did a hell of a job, kid, chasing down your dream.
Rudy: I don't care. If it doesn't produce results, it doesn't mean anything.
Father Cavanaugh: I think you'll discover that it will.
Rudy: Maybe I haven't prayed enough.
Father Cavanaugh: I'm sure that's not the problem. Praying is something we do in our time. The answers come in God's time.
Rudy: Have I done everything I possibly can? Can you help me?
Father Cavanaugh: Son, in 35 years. of religious studies... ...I've come up with only two hard, incontrovertible facts: There is a God... ...and I'm not Him.

We can count on God helping us to his steer the ship, but even with Him helping you set sail, you still need to be the captain. Rudy did everything he could, and after long last, he got into to Notre Dame. His father was about as proud as he could be, but Rudy would not quit until he was on the football team. After begging and pleading with the coach to let him on the team, the coach agrees, but warns him, if he ever ends up coming to close to messing up or does not give it his all, he will be cut just like that. One of the most common bits of leadership wisdom that any leader will bestow up on his followers is to treat every single job as you are the CEO, even if what you are doing might seem to others as simply menial. Rudy does this, and so did Cook in his quest to walk on to UGA's football team, and so did I when I first started working at N3. As opposed to wearing just a polo and khaki slacks, I would make it a point to wear a buttoned down shirt, nice dress slacks, and a blazer to work. At one point, one of my fellow workers asked me why I did so, considering were just making cold calls and never would directly interface with the prospect in person.

I did so because I wanted to dress professionally in front of management, and sure enough, who was picked as New Business Development to go on trips to conferences in San Francisco Austin, and Orlando? Me. Cook dealt with the same issue when he was trying to make the team at UGA. The others players complained that he was making them look bad because he tried so hard. One thing for sure is true in life: if you treat every job as a life-or-death situation, you will end up giving life to others because you yourself will eventually be in a leadership position.

I mentioned Greta Thunberg earlier on the book. Whether or not you agree with her position on climate change, you have to admit that what she has been able to accomplish is nothing short of amazing. You might not know this, but her whole movement got started by holding up a sign outside the Swedish Parliament that said "school strike for climate." One reason she was taken so seriously is because she was only fifteen years old; in other words, she was an at an age where she would typically be overlooked. In a TEDx Talk in Stockholm in 2018, she said, "I was diagnosed with Asperger's syndrome, OCD and selective mutism. That basically means I only speak when I think it's necessary. Now is one of those moments." Is there a moment in your own life where it is necessary for you to speak up? Can you do it even if you feel overlooked in the first place?

*

I was on the phone the other day with an acquaintance I met from LinkedIn talking about her journey as a walk-on as a college basketball player at Ole Miss. She told me that her journey got started by one of her friends trying to convince her just to practice with her and some of the girls on the team. Eventually, she agreed, and went out and practiced. What she told me on the phone a few months ago is that she was surprised to find that she could keep up with the players on the team. While she was much shorter than them, she found that she was just as good as shooting three points shots if not better than them. When you're initially overlooked, you and others around you often times draw up the conclusion that you are not good enough. When that happens to you, be thankful for it, because discouragement can be a good thing. A flower needs both shade and sun to grow; too much sun can overheat the flower causing it to die. You've read about Rudy, George Marshall, Bill McDermott, and myself being overlooked. Because we were overlooked in the first place, we are now in the position where we look

99

after others. Just remember: to look at someone to begin with, you must have sight, so why not take the steps necessary to be a sight to see?

REFERENCES

Chapter 1

1. "ZM." https://finance.yahoo.com/quote/ZM?p=ZM&.tsrc=fin-srch. Yahoo! Finance. 5/24/22.
2. *Outliers*. Malcom Gladwell. Back Bay Books. New York, NY. Page 54.
3. *Outliers*. Malcom Gladwell. Back Bay Books. New York, NY.
4. "The Big Short." Screenplay By Charles Randolph and Adam McKay. Based Upon the book by Malcom Lewis. https://s3.amazonaws.com/thescriptlab/screenplays/2015/the-big-short.pdf. 5/24/22.
5. *A First Rate Madness*. Nassir Ghaemi. Penguin Books. New York, NY. Page 15.
6. *Winners Dream: A Journey from The Corner Store to the Corner Office*. Bill McDermott. Simon & Schuster. New York. 2014.
7. *Holy Bible*. Genesis 6:1-8. Zondervan. Grand Rapids, MI Page 9.
8. "Eh Hee" AZ Lyrics. https://www.azlyrics.com/lyrics/davematthews/ehhee.html.
9. *A Return to Love: Reflections on the Principles of "A Course in Miracles."* Marianne Williamson. Ch.7, Section 3 (1992), p.190.

Chapter 2

1. *Talking to Strangers*. Malcom Gladwell. Hachette Book Group. New York, NY. 2019. Page 179.

2. "5 Reasons Why Nerds Become Highly Successful in Life." Modi Palmer Ramos. May 24th, 2022. Pucker Mob. https://www.puckermob.com/lifestyle/5-reasons-why-nerds-become-highly-successful-in-life/. 5/29/22.

3. *The Making of Robert E. Lee.* Michael Fellman. Johns Hopkins. Baltimore, MD. Page 116.

4. "The Big Short." Screenplay By Charles Randolph and Adam McKay. Based Upon the book by Malcom Lewis. https://s3.amazonaws.com/thescriptlab/screenplays/2015/the-big-short.pdf. 5/29/22.

5. *The Adventures of Tom Sawyer.* Mark Twain. Barnes & Noble. New York Pages 9-14.

6. "The Big Short." Screenplay By Charles Randolph and Adam McKay. Based Upon the book by Malcom Lewis. https://s3.amazonaws.com/thescriptlab/screenplays/2015/the-big-short.pdf. 5/29/22.

7. *George Marshall: Defender of the Republic.* David L. Roll. Dutton Caliber. 2020. New York. Pages 67 and 68.

8. *Outliers.* Gladwell. Page 30.

Chapter 3

1. "The Big Short." Screenplay By Charles Randolph and Adam McKay. Based Upon the book by Malcom Lewis. https://s3.amazonaws.com/thescriptlab/screenplays/2015/the-big-short.pdf. 5/29/22.

2. *Thinking Fast and Slow.* Daniel Kahneman. Farrar, Straus, & Giroux. New York. 2013. Page 7.

3. "The Big Short." Screenplay By Charles Randolph and Adam McKay. Based Upon the book by Malcom Lewis.

https://s3.amazonaws.com/thescriptlab/screenplays/2015/the-big-short.pdf. 5/29/22.

4. "C.H. Spurgeon: Noah's Faith, Fear, Obedience, and Salvation." Blue Letter Bible. https://www.blueletterbible.org/Comm/spurgeon_charles/sermons/2147.cfm. 5/29/22.

5. "The Big Short." Screenplay By Charles Randolph and Adam McKay. Based Upon the book by Malcom Lewis. https://s3.amazonaws.com/thescriptlab/screenplays/2015/the-big-short.pdf. 5/29/22.

6. *Lincoln on Leadership*. Donald Phillips. Warner Books. 1992. Page 88.

7. "The Big Short." Screenplay By Charles Randolph and Adam McKay. Based Upon the book by Malcom Lewis. https://s3.amazonaws.com/thescriptlab/screenplays/2015/the-big-short.pdf. 5/29/22.

8. "The Big Short." Screenplay By Charles Randolph and Adam McKay. Based Upon the book by Malcom Lewis. https://s3.amazonaws.com/thescriptlab/screenplays/2015/the-big-short.pdf. 5/29/22.

Chapter 4

1. Twain. Pages 123-127.

2. *Dopamine Nation: Finding Balance in the Age of Indulgence*. Anna Lembke. Dutton. New York, NY. Page 46.

3. "It's Dogged as Does It." Michael Shermer. February 2006. https://michaelshermer.com/sciam-columns/its-dogged-as-does-it/. 5/29/22.

4. "The Big Short." Screenplay By Charles Randolph and Adam McKay. Based Upon the book by Malcom Lewis. https://s3.amazonaws.com/thescriptlab/screen-plays/2015/the-big-short.pdf. 5/29/22.

Chapter 5

1. "The Big Short." Screenplay By Charles Randolph and Adam McKay. Based Upon the book by Malcom Lewis. https://s3.amazonaws.com/thescriptlab/screen-plays/2015/the-big-short.pdf. 5/29/22.
2. *Outliers.* Gladwell. Pages 38-42.
3. *Outliers.* Gladwell.
4. *Grit: The Story of Passion and Perseverance.* Angela Duckworth. Scribner. New York. 2016. Page ix-xi.

Chapter 6

1. Roll.
2. *The Road to Character.* David Brooks. Random House New York, NY. 2015. Page 106.
3. *From Underdog to Bulldog: My Journey as a College Football Walk-On.* Candler Cook. Lioncrest. 2019. Page 33.
4. "Bill McDermott, CEO of SAP – The Brave Ones." YouTube. June 12th, 2017. https://www.youtube.com/watch?v=on40BNZHUr4&t=1205s. 5/29/22.
5. "Rudy (1993) Movie Script." https://www.springfieldspring-field.co.uk/movie_script.php?movie=rudy. 5/29/22.
6. McDermott. Page 23-24.

7. Cook. Page 96.

Chapter 7

1. Twain. Page 4.
2. "Rudy (1993) Movie Script." https://www.springfieldspring-field.co.uk/movie_script.php?movie=rudy. 5/29/22.
3. Duckworth. Page 8.
4. Cook. Page 102-5.
5. "Identity in bipolar disorder: Self-worth and achievement." Manon L. Ironisde. Sheri L. Johnson. Charles S. Carver. Journal of Personality. Volume 88. Issue 1. Pages 45-48.
6. Roll. Page 99.

Chapter 8

1. *My Utmost for His Highest*. Oswald Chambers. Our Daily Bread Publishing. 2017.
2. *Holy Bible*. Page 987.
3. "4 Quotes Worth Reflecting On." Drew Henricks. Inc.com. https://www.inc.com/magazine/202205/tom-foster/mark-cuban-cold-email-mentor-investor.html. 5/29/22.
4. Roll. Page 112-13.
5. "Rudy (1993) Movie Script." https://www.springfieldspring-field.co.uk/movie_script.php?movie=rudy. 5/29/22.
6. Duckworth. Page 14.

Chapter 9

1. Duckworth. Page 36.
2. Duckworth. Page 23.

3. "Identity in bipolar disorder: Self-worth and achievement." Manon L. Ironisde. Sheri L. Johnson. Charles S. Carver. Journal of Personality. Volume 88. Issue 1. Pages 45-48.
4. Roll.
5. "Identity in bipolar disorder: Self-worth and achievement." Manon L. Ironisde. Sheri L. Johnson. Charles S. Carver. Journal of Personality. Volume 88. Issue 1. Pages 45-48

Chapter 10

1. "Rudy (1993) Movie Script." https://www.springfieldspringfield.co.uk/movie_script.php?movie=rudy. 5/29/22.
2. Brady, Jeff (28 August 2019). https://www.npr.org/2019/08/28/754818342/teen-climate-activist-greta-thunberg-arrives-in-new-york-after-sailing-the-atlan. *NPR.* 5/29/22.

From the Pages of *Forget Self-Help: Re-Examining the Golden Rule*

Nonetheless, when someone bears our burdens with us, often a huge weight lifts from our shoulders. Does this mean that the other person can solve the problem that the other one is going through? *No.* However, just knowing that someone cares enough to forget his *own* problems and focus on *yours* is reassuring. **—CHAPTER 1**

When people speak of having an advantage over someone, they often feel as if they have to tread on sharp glass. There is no need to do this because none of us created our own advantages. They were given to us by God. However, we do need to tread lightly on how we use our own advantages to help others. **—CHAPTER 2**

Usually, when we ourselves are in a position of power, we like to look to see how we can use it to control others instead of realizing that we need to control ourselves that much more because of the position we are now in. **—CHAPTER 2**

A man's heart is only strong when it is safe, and it is only safe when it is secured in something strong. **—CHAPTER 2**

Since none of us will see God on Earth, we face an uphill battle to show others that God truly exists.**—CHAPTER 3**

One reason that we never get to know other people is because it requires us to become vulnerable to other people. To become vulnerable not only requires work but also requires courage. Many people are unwilling to admit their blind spots or flaws. However, when this happens, a whole new world is opened up because it enables both parties to be real with each other.—**CHAPTER 4**

Without loving oneself first, it is impossible to love others. —**CHAPTER 4**

Everyone can agree though that anything worthwhile, anything worth striving for, has some element of rarity to it.—**CHAPTER 5**

When judging another person, I never look for the big moments that test their character. I look for the small ones. Big moments carry a heroic aspect to them so there is a certain selfish incentive to make sure they are carried out to fruition. Small moments, however, never get any credit. This accentuates their value. —**CHAPTER 6**

We need to be extreme. We need to be bold. We need to go all out. But we need to do this all for others, not ourselves. —**CHAPTER 6**

The best way to tell if someone is with you is to see whether a person will help you even if he knows he will get nothing in return from you. Anyone can help when there is something to gain in return; to help when there is nothing to be gained shows true love. —**CHAPTER 7**

Showing mercy toward others is not an easy task. It requires patience, humility, and an inverse style of thinking that goes against our natural selfish desires. It also requires giving up a sense of control, a sense of control we often feel like we earned in the first place. **—CHAPTER 7**

Holding someone accountable for their actions can be one of the most delicate and awkward dealings that a human being has to do for another. But in strong relationships, this happens frequently. **—CHAPTER 8**

So many times, we lash out against others when they give us advice or critique our actions. We need to realize they are doing so because they believe in us and think we are capable of greatness. **—CHAPTER 8**

When we do for others, we provide more happiness for ourselves more effectively than when we try to focus only on ourselves. The reason for this is simple: putting ourselves in another's shoes makes us forget all about our own problems. **—CHAPTER 8**

What happens when we focus less on ourselves and instead devote that energy toward others? We benefit others and also benefit ourselves. When we reach out to someone who is in need, we fulfill the words of Christ. By following the Golden Rule in our attitude, behavior, and conduct, we make the world a better place and make our own lives better too. **—CONCLUSION**

You only love someone when you are willing to sacrifice for them; without sacrifice, there is no love. **—CONCLUSION**

From the Pages of *The Criminal: The Power of An Apology*

Failing at an early age produces character, determination, and humility, all of which can never be learned without it.   If you do fail, however, it means you had the courage to take a risk, which is in itself, quite admirable – **CHAPTER 1**

Failing should be thought of like a photograph. You see it, but only for the instant in which the image was captured.   Photography can be misleading, just like failing. – **CHAPTER 1**

Failing is not failure; how you react to your failure is the indication of whether you have truly failed or not. – **CHAPTER 1**

Courage often is a result of failure in the same way that success is a result of courage; therefore, to achieve success in life, you have to overcome failure with courage. – **CHAPTER 1**

The only way to be found is to admit we are lost. – **CHAPTER 2**

We all hope; it is what we hope for that demonstrates where our true heart is. All the criminal hoped for is to be found again; in his repentance and in his character, that happened. – **CHAPTER 2**

With Christianity, the less you are in control, the more you are in control. – **CHAPTER 2**

The nice thing about knowing that Jesus died for our sins is that once we know that simple truth, our lives are transformed. Sin in no longer chasing us; we know longer have to dodge and weave to hide: we are free, but only if we admit our sin. **– CHAPTER 2**

In making yourself vulnerable to the ones you love, a foundation as solid as a rock is formed. **– CHAPTER 2**

Admitting your blind spot is a challenging thing to, but it produces a realness is relationships, because it shows the person you know that you are only human.   That humbleness opens the door for them to be humble back to you, opening the way for a deeper form of communication than you thought was possible. **– CHAPTER 2**

I often find myself trying to be perfect, and when I'm not, I find myself trying to cover up my sin when I should be doing the opposite because Christ died for me. **– CHAPTER 2**

The last thing I like to do is admit that I am wrong, but when I do, I know God is smiling; after all, it means my complete trust is in him. **– CHAPTER 2**

To God however, beauty means admitting we are broken and lost, needing to pick up God's rhythms to regain it. Whatever we do is not enough because we have all fallen short, so very short of his Glory. Only in the cross, can we regain that beauty. **– CHAPTER 2**

The opposite of sarcasm is vulnerability. You can tell when a man is strong when he is more attuned to the latter rather than the former. **– CHAPTER 3**

Without integrity, a person is empty. The emptiness comes from that person's lack of respect for reality; in life, reality accounts for everything that is worthwhile. **– CHAPTER 4**

To make a difference, we have to make a change. The reason for this is rather simple: we are all fallen—in need of his saving grace—**CHAPTER 4**

It is only when we hide our sin that we get into trouble. Admitting your trouble is the surest way to get out of trouble in Christianity. **– CHAPTER 4**

Being honest doesn't require you to be good-looking, smart, or clever, it only requires showing your authentic self to the world. Chances are, if you are honest, people will appreciate you more, listen to you more, and value you more. The reason for this is simple: you will now be set apart in a rare class. **– CHAPTER 4**

To take it learning even further, one has to learn from anybody and everybody, even the flawed. In doing so, your life will be changed, and once your life is changed, you will change others. **– CHAPTER 5**

Only when we admit that we are less, and He is more, will we be found. The reason for this simple: admitting that we are less doesn't make us *less*, it makes us *more*. **– CHAPTER 5**

With power, often comes pride. That pride is not from above, but down below. The only thing we need to be prideful of is what Jesus did for us on the cross. It was the opposite of prideful. Because of this, it was definition of powerful. **– CHAPTER 5**

Jesus never seeks earthly might. To be a king is to be rich, powerful, carry a good name, and have lots of servants. I guess Jesus never got the memo. For him, power was in being *with* us, not *over* us. **– CHAPTER 5**

Most people are too proud to learn, but the most impactful of people always take the position that in order to impact people, you can never learn enough. **– CHAPTER 5**

We're blessed in that when Jesus said, "It is finished", what it meant for us is that it was only getting started. Through his death on the cross, we could start to love again, start to matter again, but most of all, we could start to heal again. In healing again, we can start to live again. And we are doubly blessed in that most leaders close their doors. Most famous people try to avoid the paparazzi and fans. Not Jesus though. He told us he would be with us until the end of the age. **– CHAPTER 5**

We are all fake, all lost, void of anything worthwhile without the blood of Jesus. We all need blood in order to survive. Why live only to survive, why not live to thrive? We can, but only with the blood of Jesus. Only his blood is pure, that is for certain. **– CHAPTER 6**

When we repent, we are secure. It's a security that is much more comforting than a 401K or a seat-belt in a car. It's a security that transcends all understanding, and once you have it, all you want to do is pass it on. After all, to give that security is to give life. And it's not just life on this earth, it's life everlasting. **– CHAPTER 6**

I need Jesus' blood just as I need oxygen, food, water, and shelter. Without it, I can never survive, never thrive. Without it I am a nobody, I can achieve nothing. With it, I am not only powerful, I am free. **– CHAPTER 6**

We're often taught to present our best self to the world even though deep down we know this is not for the best. **– CHAPTER 6**

You can tell how much someone believes in the cross by how open they are about their own sin. **– CHAPTER 6**

Thankfulness shouldn't be situation-based because difficult times have a way of shaping us in a stronger, more effective way than a seemingly encouraging time. It's more challenging to grow when things are going well. When you're at the very bottom, upward is the only direction you can go. **– CHAPTER 6**

To be thankful isn't to walk around with a smile on your face all the time. Jesus didn't have a smile on his face when he was crucified. After all, didn't he cry out, "why have you forsaken me?" He did have the wherewithal to trust God during that time, however. When you trust in God during the toughest of times, He credits that as thankfulness. **– CHAPTER 8**

For me, gratitude can frame meaningless drudgery into meaningful opportunities."

Disciple is the root word of discipline. So why is discipline seen as an *extremely* negative word and disciple as an extremely *positive* word? **– CHAPTER 9**

It might seem like a paradox, but you want to try to be a person that no one wants to be around because when he leaves your presence they are immediately disappointed by the decreased level of character and encouragement they are now forced to be around in terms of dealing with other people. **– CHAPTER 9**

I challenge the people I respect, but to those who have neither the capacity nor ability to change, I am silent. **– CHAPTER 9**

The criminal serves as a guide to us all. He's humble, yet unafraid, clever, without the usual pretentiousness; but most of all, he is loyal, and in his loyalty, he became the first convert to Christianity; in doing so, he joined Jesus in paradise forever. **– CONCLUSION**

From the Pages of *He Spoke with Authority: Get, then Give the Advantage of Confidence*

It made me realize two things: to be happy for another person's success doesn't make you *less* of a person, it makes you *more* of a person. It also made me realize that the common perception that a true friend is one who is with you during the worst of times is wrong. A friend who is with you during the best of your times is truly there for you for he is not jealous, but happy for you, showing true love. - **CHAPTER 1**

All of us should have the utmost confidence in ourselves for one primary reason: what Jesus did for us on the cross. Once we realize that, indeed, we are made perfect by His actions, we can shake off all the insecurities that hold us back and start to live for Him. It's tough for us to comprehend this because we live in such a merit-based society; luckily for, our merit was earned by Jesus' blood on the cross. Nothing else can make us more whole or secure. – **CHAPTER 1**

People are going to doubt you if you possess the courage to do anything great. Let them do so: chances are they are jealous that you have the guts and talent to try. – **CHAPTER 1**

It's okay to think that you are capable of greatness. That's not a sin in God's eyes. Just make sure you are using your talents and so forth for God's glory, not just your own. The scariest scenario for the Devil is to have a confident God-fearing human carrying out the Lord's work. The Devil is not at all scared of insecure Christ followers; in fact, that's who he takes advantage of the most. – **CHAPTER 2**

Don't let others lead you down your own path; let God do that; God knew you first. **– CHAPTER 2**

We can bring heaven here on earth, but only when we display confidence in ourselves. Sitting on the sidelines is futile. **– CHAPTER 2**

Do yourself a favor: let the force of confidence get you moving. When you do, you will move others and, in the process, be moved yourself. **– CHAPTER 2**

For parents to stifle their child's optimism is to not only stifle their own dreams, but the dreams of others. The reason for this is simple: once one achieves their own dreams, they often help others to achieve their own dreams; at least the great ones do. **– CHAPTER 2**

Protectors are able to protect us because the security they have in themselves; they refuse to be insecure because they know they have to be secure for others. **- CHAPTER 2**

The Bible tells us that to much has been given, much is expected; go into your day knowing that you have been entrusted with much and it is all for His glory, not just for your own pleasure. With this new way of thinking, you'll find that your pleasure becomes His glory. Ultimately, you know your faith is strong when you say "thank you" to God, and God says, "no, *thank you.*" This means that your purpose in life and His will are one in the same. **– CHAPTER 2**

There is nothing more noble than sticking up for someone else when they have been wronged. There is one characteristic that a human being must have to do this: confidence. Sticking up for yourself is easy, but to stick up for another human being shows a blend of both unselfishness and confidence which the mother and father of what Christianity is all about. **– CHAPTER 3**

You can't always be safe and confident at the same time. And chances are if you are too confident, you are doing something that is too safe. **- CHAPTER 3**

When you're the only one that can stick up for yourself, do so with courage and you may just find the respect of the people who have tried to trample you down. At the very least, they may find some empathy for the situation. **– CHAPTER 3**

Security in oneself leads to security in the other person. It shows that you are humble, not so much putting the weight of the world in yourself, but ultimately others. If you're secure with yourself, you'll find yourself reaching out to make sure other people are secure with themselves. In doing so, you'll become that much more secure with yourself. **- CHAPTER 3**

When you find yourself sticking up for people more and more, you know that you are growing more and more confident; the insecure, however, only stick up for themselves. **– CHAPTER 3**

Other's affliction should affect all of us, and when it does, you know you're confident in your own skin. **- CHAPTER 3**

While it is noble to turn the other cheek, when another person is hurting you so much to the point where you have trouble living, it is not only okay to stick up for yourself, but God wants you to do so; he wants you to be strong so you can do His work. **– CHAPTER 3**

Getting out of abusive relationships is hard, but necessary. When you're in an abusive relationship, it is impossible to carry out God's will the best you can because in the back of your mind you're filled with all the trauma of the abusive relationship. **– CHAPTER 3**

Whatever seems unlikely, improbable, even if something has never happened before, it can happen through God. Is it okay to be nervous knowing that you are chosen by God to do his work? Yes, but just know that by putting your confidence in Him, you will in turn be more confident, being able to accomplish anything for Him. **– CHAPTER 4**

Once we have confidence in Him, he gives us all the confidence we need to do His work. God wants you to be confident; He knows that without it, the mission he has set before us will never be accomplished. **– CHAPTER 4**

When we look out for others, our confidence shows in plain light and cannot be hidden. God gave us confidence so we could save others just as He saved us on the cross. Once this shift of perspective in your thinking happens, you will be bolder, thus changing more lives. — **CHAPTER 4**

Confidence is like centrifugal force; it is never ceasing, it always extends to the receiver and back to the giver. It doesn't just unlock doors, it tears them down off its hinges so it will be easier for the next person walk through; or, better yet, run through. — **CHAPTER 4**

 Confident people often sacrifice themselves so that the rest of us cannot only live but live well; these people aren't so bad after all, for they lived as Jesus lived.; they sacrifice just as Jesus sacrificed.- **CHAPTER 4**

When you're vulnerable with someone, there is a connection that cannot be broken. In laying down all your cards, you'll discover that you have the winning hand. The reason you win is by allowing the other person to see you clearly for the first time—allowing them to assist you when you need assistance, cry with you when you feel you need comfort, and help you stand when you feel as if you cannot bear your own weight. — **CHAPTER 5**

To be vulnerable is to be real, and in that vulnerability, you are strong. - **CHAPTER 5**

Intimacy is like that tough conversation that you don't want to have: you dread it, during it you're scared and frightened, but afterwards you're telling yourself: I can't wait to come back for more. The next time though, you dread it less, thus enabling you to be even more intimate; once again; after you've experienced it, you come back for more. - **CHAPTER 5**

What does having a mentor say about somebody? Well, ultimately, it shows that they are both confident and humble—two words that rarely go together. It shows that you are humble enough to feel that you *need* to improve and confident enough that you *can* improve. - **CHAPTER 6**

Confidence leads to empathy because of the security you have in yourself. With that security, you can give it to others who need it. – **CHAPTER 6**

To be a strong Christian, you must emit a different type of electricity to others. It's a type of electricity that only comes from confidence. You'll often find that once you emit that electricity toward others, you will get just as much back. – **CHAPTER 7**

Real love is not silent; it speaks to us in a way we are not used to hearing; therefore, there is no way to mute it like we turn like we mute TV commercials. Real love is strong, bold, courageous, and confident; it teaches us to dare in its daringness. – **CHAPTER 8**

From the Pages of *Mrs. Dubose's Last Wish*

We all suffer from time to time in our lives, some more than others. It's how we react to that suffering that separates the winners from the losers. – **CHAPTER 1**

The strongest predictor of success is the amount of suffering one is willing to embrace. – **CHAPTER 1**

To want to fight after enduring so much pain, you have to not only outlast until the final bell rings, but you also have to overcome trials and tribulations that seem like they will go on forever. – **CHAP-TER 1**

When we are on the ground and can't stand up, we tend to think God has forgotten about us. This couldn't be further from the truth because God uses painful experiences not only to build us up, but also others around us. – **CHAPTER 1**

When our complete trust is in God, we have no choice but to thank God for whatever happens, knowing firmly that *He*, and not *we*, has the best handle on our lives. – **CHAPTER 1**

Whatever you are going through at the present time, just know that—believe it or not—God knows what you are going through, and, better yet, he knows what you have to do to get through to the finish line. – **CHAPTER 2**

Whatever you are going through, fear should not have a place in your heart because The Lord is by your side just as a best friend is with you through your worst times, and He is your number one cheerleader during your best times, or, in this digital age, the first one to post your success on social media. He is not afraid to sacrifice for you, even if it means going through a painful, gruesome death on a wooden cross for you.   He's already gone through that pain, so that you can have pain no more. - **CHAPTER 2**

When someone tells you that they want you to see something, they're telling you that because they feel as if you have not noticed something that they think would be beneficial for you to see; more than likely, something to make you grow. - **CHAPTER 2**

When I think of someone who is worthy of respect, I immediately think of someone who is hard on themselves.   To earn the respect of all, one must be hard on himself. The moment he lets go of this plight, is the moment he begins to lose the respect of many, if not all. - **CHAPTER 3**

I've realized that the most influential don't mind suffering themselves, but if they're even put in a position where they can alleviate another's suffering, they'll do so every single time, often in a hurry. - **CHAPTER 3**

When we love unconditionally—without getting anything back in return—we end up getting just as much back, if not more.   The quicker others pain becomes yours is the barometer of how sensitive you are, and, contrary to popular belief, being sensitive is not a sign of weakness, but strength. - **CHAPTER 3**

Suffering isn't easy and *choosing* to suffer is even harder. But in life, we must choose to suffer if we ever want anything accomplished. – **CHAPTER 4**

It is alright for us to pray to God to alleviate our suffering, but only if it furthers his kingdom or will. If you can do that, you know you are on the path to a close relationship with The Lord. - **CHAPTER 4**

If what you're about to attempt doesn't scare you, what you're attempting to do is not of insignificance. Signs on the highway show significant landmarks such as places to eat, stay, and be entertained. Let what you're striving after show the signs of significance as well. — **CHAPTER 4**

Only when you begin to choose to suffer from time to time do you know your faith is catching on. If you find yourself seeking pleasure all the time instead of pain, check yourself because not only do sacrifice and suffering start with the same letter, they both bring a smile to God. — **CHAPTER 6**

When you're suffering, you naturally think that first and foremost you must dig yourself out of a hole, when in actuality, digging other people out of a hole can prove to be much more effective for alleviating that suffering — **CHAPTER 6**

In many ways we can't choose the fate that God has given us. Some of us are born tall, some of us are born short, some of us white, some of us black. What we can do, however, is react to what God has given us because he has given us free-will. We are not robots programmed by God; we have choices. Whatever problems you are going through, know that in the end, you have a choice as to how you will react to it. — **CHAPTER 6**

Our first inclination is look out for ourselves when we are suffering, and, when we do so, it often causes us to forget to look out for the needs of others. Christ, on the other hand, got hurt on the cross so he could *help* people. He didn't have to do so, but he wanted to make us whole again. – **CHAPTER 6**

Sometimes, the reason God wants us to suffer is to get that big part of us that is off the track back on the rails. He does this because this is the only way we will be able to see what we are doing wrong. Are you wise enough to realize this?   I hope so. – **CHAPTER 6**

Life is very reactionary; those who react with the most bravery during the most harrowing times are the ones who are remembered. In debates, politicians, are taught by their debate coaches not to react in a negative way even if their competitors are trying to get under their skin. – **CHAPTER 6**

From the Pages of *Listen Up: Seek Enough Advice and One Day You'll Be Giving It*

Too often, we are too arrogant to know that we have much to learn in this world. Too often, we assume that we have a grasp on things, when in actuality, we have no clue what is going on. **– CHAPTER 1**

Why is listening and receiving advice so hard for many of us? It is as if we feel insulted when we receive help or are forced to listen. It is one thing to listen to advice from someone who is older than us, but to listen to advice from someone who are our own age or younger than us seems unfathomable. Oftentimes, the best of us feel humble enough to receive advice and listen, improving with every encounter. **– CHAPTER 1**

Truly being open to guidance doesn't mean that you don't know the answer, it means you are humble enough to admit that there's a possibility, as slight as it could be, that you don't know the answer. Having that type of mentality is the only way to grow, because you only grow when you are tested, and in order to pass a test, you must listen. **- CHAPTER 1**

You never do know when you might receive a lesson from someone you deem less educated than yourself however high and mighty you think you are, so rather than close your ears, keep them open and you just might find that you'll advance. Call it wild, but you just might advance behind your wildest dreams. **– CHAPTER 1**

To understand someone, you've got to listen; you've got to be paying close attention to what the other is going through more than what you are going through. Environmentalists often say tread lightly and leave no trace. Understanding someone can be phrased in the opposite manner: tread heavily where they have tread, then you'll be able to make a trace on their hearts & in their lives. - **CHAPTER 2**

Being skilled will take you far, but if you get to the point where you are so skilled that you don't believe you can need aid to better yourself, you are in treacherous territory. - **CHAPTER 3**

Whether we'd like to admit it or not, we're drawn to people who listen to us. Usually the people who listen to us tend to be in a lower or similar status. That's why, when someone we perceive as powerful than us takes the time and effort to listen to us, we appreciate that instance more than a normal instance. God, in his mighty power, never fails to listen to us. If God never fails to listen to us, why do we constantly fail to listen to others? **– CHAPTER 3**

I realize many of my writing is of a very personal tone, especially on the subject of my fight with mental illness, but when I realized that my writing was having an impact on people in a positive way, all the embarrassment and shame went away… God gave me the ability to think, be creative, and write in order to help people whether they be Christian or not. I take great pride in being part of God's team, and it only happened because I listened to his call. **– CHAPTER 4**

Listening can be oh so difficult because of our pride. We like to think that we know it all, more often than not, and to receive advice is seen as something weak, lacking true purpose.
– CHAPTER 4

Our Lord our God tells us to live boldly, to take a risk, to surprise many including ourselves. How does one gain the capacity to surprise oneself? I've learned, that more often than not, in order to have the capacity to surprise ourselves, we must look at life as someone who is at the bottom of a swimming pool. No matter how hard we try to stay at the bottom, we seem to always come up with force. Trusting that God gave you the force to do anything seems incomprehensible is something that must always been implanted in the back of your mind. **– CHAPTER 5**

A stud's purpose is to form a vertical structural load. It can also be non load-bearing. Studs hold in place windows, doors, interior finish, exterior sheathing or siding, insulation and utilities, but, if you ask a contractor, what the most important thing a stud does is to give shape to a building. Finding a person who shapes you is the person who God wants you to be with. **– CHAPTER 6**

To be truly known by the other starts with the other listening and absorbing information to realize not only what other makes the person tick, but what moves the other person—what makes the other person not only get out of bed, but also keeps the person from going back to bed in the middle of the day.
– CHAPTER 6

Gardeners and contractors may not seem like they would at all be a similar profession, but they are both building something—something that is meant to last and be used. Both professions also require listening. Not listening in the sense of hearing but listening in the sense of knowing what their admirers or habitants want. If they're good at they're profession, their wants begin to be innate; they naturally want to build a foundation that lasts until eternity. – **CHAPTER 6**

When you think of a leader who is adaptable, you think of someone who is not only calm under pressure, but someone who is not naïve to different circumstances; they can assure their followers that no matter what, their plan will work whatever is thrown their way. – **CHAPTER 7**

When people think of arrogance, they often judge someone based on the fact if this person brags a lot. I, on the other hand, look to see if they are humble enough to admit that they in fact do not know it all. – **CHAPTER 7**

Luckily, with God's word, we have instructions on how to make every decision in life. All we have to do is listen to him and trust that even if it is the harder path, listening to His choice makes us live with purpose. – **CHAPTER 8**

I've sometimes wondered why I use so many quotations in my books from others, and, at the beginning of my books have included two or three from each chapter. I've come to the conclusion it is because, above all, people tell us quotes and share quotes with us to encourage, to inspire. – **CHAPTER 9**

Find people that challenge you. When you do this, you'll often find the challenges you face in the future are less difficult because the training this person has put you through. The weak surround themselves with people who are too timid to stick up to them, while the strong get the feeling that no future battle should be left untested. **– CHAPTER 9**

By admitting that I was not only wrong in one area of my actions but could have improved my area in another area actions, I just got a lot better. If we think about it, when someone critiques our actions, instead of our first thought being to say that they're wrong, we might ask them for additional things we need to work on because we might feel as if they are tip-toeing around us to make sure our feelings don't get hurt if they brought up additional issues. – **CHAPTER 9**

Leaders are on the unquenchable quest to get better. The best CEO's make performance reviews two-sided instead of the boss just focusing on the employee is performing. This way, the CEO gets better, and when the CEO gets better, he/she can lead more effectively. **– CHAPTER 9**

Music has a way of lifting us up in a way that nothing else quite can. It moves us, challenges us; in short, it is the both the glue and motor that binds and pushes us to pursue life in a different way we never thought was possible. We listen to music; not only to hear the instruments, but to hear the lyrics teach just as a school-teacher lectures at a podium. Will we listen to them? Are we both humble and strong enough to do just that? **– CHAPTER 10**

Age is not only the exact prerequisite for wisdom, but experience. A young person can draw from experiences just as an elder can. It doesn't happen very often, but when it does, you better being willing to listen and be humble, for one of the definitions of humble is ranking low in a hierarchy or scale. Can you make yourself low to become high? **– CHAPTER 10**

My best contributions to the world have started with listening, while my failures have often been the direct result of an inability to listen. **– CHAPTER 11**

The strong don't mind feeling as if they don't have to be in control. Control to them means controlling themselves first. From there, they feel like they have a handle on every situation that arises. **– CHAPTER 12**

Our eyes swell when we are filled with emotion. The only way that can happen to us is if we feel listened to. When we are listened to, we feel that we are cared for, and, when we are cared for, we know are loved. **– CHAPTER 12**

You feel a void most in your life not when you cannot have the latest dress, car, or house, but when you lose something that is dear to you. This is why relationships are so much more important than things. **– CHAPTER 12**

When you receive and or give meaningful advice, a bond is formed between both individuals that can't be broken. It's as if you become on the same team, one hand lifting up the other towards a common goal. **– CHAPTER 12**

From the Pages of *Alone at the Lunch Table: How to Rise from Rejection*

You're not accepted until you are rejected. **– CHAPTER 1**

All of us in our own lives face times where we can or cannot earn admission into an institution, get the job we want to get, or be in the relationship we want to be in. If you do get denied, we have no authority to be angry, or depressed because of one reason: we don't know what is best for us; only God knows that. **– CHAPTER 1**

Sometimes, when God tells you no, he is really telling you yes, for a no to you now might mean a yes to you later on. It all depends on the work God has in store for you. Sometimes, what seems like a defeat is really just the start—the start of something great. **– CHAPTER 2**

How awesome is it that God trusts us to do His work and doesn't do it alone? When you delegate, you uplift; when you feel as though you are the only person skilled enough to do the task and don't ask for help, you discourage. When the game is tied in the 9th inning, everyone wants to be the person the coach calls on to pinch-hit for the pitcher and get the job done. God could do it himself, easily, but he knows everyone wants a challenge, which gives you an opportunity to shine. With Jesus' blood, we already shine, but God wants our life to have purpose. Delegating leads to others shining, which leads to purpose. Life throws curveballs at us all the time, but if your purpose is His will, you'll break that tie. **– CHAPTER 2**

Detaching yourself from the situation and looking at things from an objective instead of a subjective point of view is the first step to getting over your rejection. **– CHAPTER 3**

I often takes things personally when I don't get a job I wanted. This again, forces me to step backward instead of going forward. It sounds cliché, but whatever that thing you didn't get was not meant for you in the first place; it turns out that it wouldn't advance His kingdom.   It's easier said than done but detach immediately after rejection and you'll find that it is much easier to deal with. **– CHAPTER 3**

Often times, when get rejected, we think we are being put down, when in actuality, as a result of the rejection, we could be lifted higher. **– CHAPTER 3**

Have you thought about something in your own life that you *must* have?   One must make sure that what *you* want aligns with what God wants.   The Devil is very clever. Wanting what seems to be a Godly thing can often become worshipping an idol. **– CHAPTER 4**

How do you start winning more arguments? I'll give you this one tip: when you find yourself losing an argument, the faster you denounce your stance and admit you're wrong, the more arguments you will win in the future. The reason for this is your thinking will be sharper and you won't find yourself making the same mistake or succumbing to the same fallacy in a future argument. **– CHAPTER 4**

Aggression, in combination with a deft touch, has served many a leader well.   One could say Jesus, the ultimate leader, possessed both in abundance. **– CHAPTER 4**

For the commoner, they believe that people want something they can't have. This technically is true. What I've found over the past few years though, however, is that playing hard to get rarely works out in the end. **– CHAPTER 5**

The biggest challenge we face as humans is the challenge to dare to be different. **– CHAPTER 6**

When we pick up the phone and call someone, ultimately, we don't know if they are going to pick up on the other end.   Still, in my opinion, it's worth making that call and reaching out because you never know if that person will help you reach your dreams. **– CHAPTER 6**

When you want something that another person has, show the other person you want it and more often than not, it will become yours. Sounds pretty simple, but in our world of email, text message, and social media, it is not. **– CHAPTER 6**

Be careful when you look down on someone, thinking that they are behind you. I've found that people who appear in your rearview mirror can enter your blind spot sooner than you think, and, while you can't see them anymore and think that they now in your blind spot, you'll be remiss to realizing that the positions have switched; you're now in *their* blind spot because they're ahead of you. They'll stay ahead of you because, unlike you, they're not looking down on anyone and are instead, zooming ahead. **– CHAPTER 7**

From the Pages of *When I See It: Belief in the Uncertainty*

"Laughter dampens our woes in a way that not only stops the pain, but gives us a chance to learn from it, thus enabling us to be stronger the next time." **– CHAPTER 2**

"Shift your reason for happiness based on *other's* happiness instead of your *own*, and you will be more fulfilled; I guarantee it." **– CHAPTER 2**

"When you're given something, you've got to pass it… pass it on, pass it around, or pass it backwards. Not to do so is not only unappreciative, but also an insult to God." **– CHAPTER 2**

"When I look at the happiest of people, they are most happy when another succeeds, not themselves." **– CHAPTER 2**

"It's not just that when one door closes, another opens, often times you'll see that when your door opens, you'll have the opportunity to open that same door for others— creating an environment that never could have happened if that original door hadn't closed. Having a door closed only means God is going to present you with an opportunity to open more doors for others—and Him—in the future." **– CHAPTER 3**

"We are often fearful of what we don't know because fear is often born out of ignorance; the worst part of this is that it can lead to

quick judgment—most of the time that judgment being wrong.” —
CHAPTER 3

“How is it that we fail to see people for who they really are more often than not? Is it pride, is it pain? Or insecurity? As human beings, we are all so different, but nonetheless so similar in the fact that we often succumb to the mistake of rushing judgment on one another, and even if we don’t rush that judgment, we often make the mistake of judging one another on inconsequential aspects of our life instead of things that matter.” **– CHAPTER 3**

“Compromising yourself is easy in times of trouble, but ultimately, there’s always only one side that’s right in disagreement, and that side is truth; to live the truth might mean sacrificing something, but in sacrificing that something, you’ll find that you gain true honor and dignity—which could have never come without the sacrifice.” **– CHAPTER 3**

“The cover—or the outside—distracts us from seeing what’s on the inside more often than not even though it contains no content—or, nothing to learn from. When people refer to what percentage of a book they’ve read, they often describe their progress in the number of pages read. They’re telling you how much content they have gotten through; only then can they truly judge a book. Judge people in the same way. Count the pages you’ve read before you start drawing conclusions.” **– CHAPTER 3**

“Layers in a cake can be challenging to read because if you look from the top down, you can’t see that there are even layers in the first place; it just seems like there is consistency in whatever it is you're looking at. But it you see the cake at eye level, you'll soon see a cake for what it's really worth—the whole picture. To see the whole picture, you must be at eye-level, meaning that you're willing to look at the cake in the same way it glances back at you. In the same way, humans must look at each other in the eye; they must make eye contact. Only then can you see the other person in their true light." **– CHAPTER 3**

"Walking with God also means that you are willing to take a risk; sometimes that risk may involve you looking like a complete fool to others. If that's the case don't sweat it, for a fool to humans is often just the person God uses most to carry out His will." **– CHAPTER 4**

"It's interesting for me to look back on my own life and realize what has happened because certain things didn't happen. It reiterates to me that God had a plan for my life, and He knows not only how to shape it but direct it as well." **– CHAPTER 4**

"When we hesitate, we are telling the thing or someone that we don't want them—that they're not important in our life. When we have a chance to do God's will and don't act on it, we are telling Him that he is not the number one priority in our life. This disappoints God more than anything, because ultimately, He knows what's best for us." **– CHAPTER 4**

"It was time to go into the world and see where I could leave my mark. My depression had ended now that I had finally seen some light, but what was I to do with my light? When you're an occasional runner, tying your shoes to go out and run is the hardest part;

for me, it was time to tie my shoes. Learning how to tie one's shoes is something we learn how to do as a child, but the more and more we live, often times, the more and more we forget how to do this simple act. We're scared of what might happen if we fail; or, are we more afraid of what will happen if we succeed? Whatever it is, tying one's shoes is difficult, but with the Lord's help—and with His purpose in mind—we can do it each and every day." **– CHAP-TER 4**

"I've learned that the outside is here today and gone tomorrow, but the inside of each one of us is what really counts, for the inside is what creates our outward actions which affect other's insides." **– CHAPTER 4**

"It's difficult to realize that God is in control, but when we do, we have a better avenue to live out His will because deep down we always know that He wants what's best for us. During the moment this type of thinking can be challenging to say the least. People often say that patience is a virtue; what it is as well is a test—a test of your faith in God." **– CHAPTER 5**

"For me personally, along with my many other flaws, I admit that I might be one of the most impatient people on the planet. Atlanta traffic drives me crazy, slow play on the golf course ahead of me is irksome, but most of all, when I want something in my life to happen and God doesn't provide it right then and there, I'm frustrated; I think He doesn't get it. Little do I know that God does get—much better than I do, in fact." **– CHAPTER 5**

"It reminds me of us shooing away God in our own lives; we can tell God to go away all we want, but He has this unfathomable ability to always watch over us even when we tell him to go away. Having God in your life is like getting super glue on your hands; He—or it—can just never seem to go away. When we cling to God, he holds on even tighter to show us we are firmly in His grasp." —
CHAPTER 5

"Entrepreneurs who make a lot of money are so successful because they are able to think outside of the box. Thinking outside the box means the perimeter is going to bigger than simply thinking inside the box. It's a risk, and it ultimately takes more effort, but in the end, it's the only way to achieve success. When you think outside the box, and don't judge a book by its cover, paradoxically, you are able to see within a person; you're able to see them for who they truly are." **– CHAPTER 7**

"Beauty is found from within because our actions are ultimately the only thing we have control over. That's the gift of free-will. The cross is the most important thing in Christianity, but once your sins are atoned for, God doesn't want you just to pray all day and sing and thank Him for it, he wants you to be a man after His own heart and spread the Gospel. He wants you to do all these things in response to that great gift you were given." **– CHAPTER 7**

"It's interesting how unselfish acts often pay dividends for us in the future; it's almost as if God sees where our heart is, appreciates it, and rewards us for our self-denial." **– CHAPTER 6**

"In the same vein, it's an interesting point to wander why God made us in the first place.   An answer you might normally get to that question is that He was lonely; but that isn't it.   Since God is all powerful, omnipotent, and perfect, he doesn't *need* anything.   It's the same choice married parents make when they decide to have children: they do so out of love—an unselfish love that transcends all understanding.   Not only did our God come down from heaven to atone for our sins, but He also created us in the first place and allows us to have a relationship with Him." **– CHAPTER 6**

"A day spent without encouraging others is a day wasted; people need you to be that agent of God in their life; there is no greater impact on your life than to impact others." **– CHAPTER 6**

"In order to start a relationship—whether it be romantic or simply friendship—there has to be a sense of permanence that will always be there. Without that, relationships cannot form properly—or at all." **– CHAPTER 6**

"Jesus wants us to dream like we used to dream when we were children. Only when we do so will we accomplish the will of the Father in heaven.   Early on in our childhood, all of us had dreams; many of us forget them when we grow older. We forget them because we lose our childlike faith that *anything* can happen with God. We start listening to the naysayers, we start to let the harsh world bring us down, but most of all, we become pessimistic and then start to believe, that even with God's help, the unthinkable can't happen. That's why we need children around us; that's why we need to become *like* children." **– CHAPTER 6**

"In many ways, it is how God appears to us. We can only see Him when we need Him the most. We have free-will, but He is still guiding our steps. We should know that God is always within ear shot, even if we are miles from Him on a rainy today. He said He would be with us—always. The word always has a sense of permanence that no other word in the English language has. It's both final and complete." **– CHAPTER 7**

"The cross is the most important thing in Christianity, but once your sins are atoned for, God doesn't want you just to pray all day and sing and thank Him for it, he wants you to be a man after His own heart and spread the Gospel. He wants you to do all these things in response to that great gift you were given." **– CHAPTER 8**

"To truly empathize with someone, more often than not means that you want them to have a *different* outcome. You want things to change for the better for them. And you want to be part of that avenue for change." **– CHAPTER 8**

From The Pages of *After the Shampoo: Conditioned for Excellence*

Your parents are very important. They are literally the first people that condition your future behavior. **– CHAPTER 1**

The absolute worst thing that can happen in life is to be conditioned by someone who is good or great—incorrectly thinking in the back of your mind the whole time that they were excellent. **– CHAPTER 1**

When I think of the most ingrateful people in my life, I think of people who feel like they deserve everything. **– CHAPTER 1**

The most arrogant people I have met in my life aren't the ones who didn't brag about themselves; they are the ones who were unwilling to listen and unwilling to apologize. **– CHAPTER 2**

The most successful people in life leverage off other people's success instead of being jealous of them, knowing full well that the momentum of that other's success will lead to them their own success. **– CHAPTER 2**

Never let someone else's success become your own defeat. **– CHAPTER 2**

You see, the more attention we get in life, when that attention gets directed towards someone else, our first reaction is naturally to feel jealous. If this happens to you, don't beat yourself up about it, but realize that you must turn that jealousy into encouragement. This way it's a win-win situation for both sides. **– CHAPTER 2**

In physics, a lever amplifies an input force to provide a greater output force, which is said to provide leverage. The ratio of the output force to the input force is the mechanical advantage of the lever. The mechanical advantage of a lever is the ratio of the load the lever overcomes and the effort a person or system applies to the lever to overcome some load or resistance. In simple words and as per the formula, it's the ratio of load and effort. Are you going to let the other person's success push you forward or push you back? **– CHAPTER 2**

How do you know if someone has made a big impact on this earth? The easiest way to see if this has happened is if someone says a person—who never said the quote in the first place—said that quote. **– CHAPTER 3**

There's a reason why people have misattributed these quotes to these people: they are more famous than the person who originally said it, thus making it more powerful of a quote. **– CHAPTER 3**

Throughout this book, I encourage you, the reader, to be conditioned not by good, not by great, but by excellent role models. I've got a question for you, though: how much more can you grow as person and in your walk with God if you can take the advice of people you don't like or don't respect? True, they might not have as good of as advice as the excellent, but you still might be able to grow from them. **– CHAPTER 3**

When giving advice, keep in mind that what you are about to propose to the other person is something new, something foreign. When you give someone a new food to try, you don't give them a whole spoonful, but only a bite. This is the way you should go about giving advice. – **CHAPTER 3**

The old can teach the young and the young can teach the old. – **CHAPTER 3**

All of us, no matter how successful we become, need encouragement. – **CHAPTER 3**

To condition someone, you must both challenge and encourage at an equal rate. When one gets in front of the other, excellence never happens. – **CHAPTER 3**

Oftentimes we cannot know God's ways; we cannot see them. But, we have to always keep in mind that he can see us. It must be this way in order for Him to condition us, which in turn brings us along. – **CHAPTER 3**

As human beings, we are naturally conditioned to seek the approval of fellow man. All of us like to fit in, but at the same time, all of seek to be excellent. I've noticed that to be excellent, you have to sacrifice your incessant desire to fit in. – **CHAPTER 4**

As Williamson says, liberate yourself from your own fear. When you do so, others will follow suit. You will raise the bar for all. Excellence has a way of causing more excellence in the same way a virus spreads; it can truly be exponential. – **CHAPTER 4**

Dare to be the first one to do something; in doing so, you'll surprise many maybe even yourself. If you do something that has already been done before, the chances of you being remembered by ages to come go down significantly. If you're not consistently pushing yourself to be the first, you may as well not even attempt what you are doing, for it is in vain. **– CHAPTER 4**

When someone above you, with more experience and wisdom than you encourages you, it is impossible to forget it; we're conditioned to not be taken seriously. **– CHAPTER 4**

Often times, when I think of my relationship with God, when he causes something to happen or not happen in my life, I realize that he has complete control of it—much more control of it then I have … Because of this, he is able to bring me along. **– CHAPTER 5**

To this day, the success I have had in writing, my technology sales career, and the education reform that I am working on currently, is due to the fact that I am not afraid to get people's opinion on matters. I'm constantly asking for advice; that's what my 6th book is about: being humble enough to seek advice. When you do this, you can become a subject matter expert on any topic even if you don't technically have a PhD in it. **– CHAPTER 5**

To become excellent, you must remember that if someone is critiquing you they think you are capable of something special—something to be remembered. Usually, when we don't hear criticism, we are happy; it I as if we did nothing wrong; I encourage us to do the opposite: we must seek out criticism in order to keep getting better. When you don't hear any, rather than be delighted, have the wherewithal to think that someone might not be taking you seriously. – **CHAPTER 5**

True, our present and future actions are dictated by our past actions, but at the same time, we have free will—we have the choice in which our destiny will be shaped. – **CHAPTER 5**

To be truly excellent, we must not be afraid to decline certain things, even if that thing be our very life. – **CHAPTER 5**

In order to influence, we must be influenced first. – **CHAPTER 5**

Dreaming is necessary when you're an underdog, and because you're forced to dream, versus knowing you'll achieve success all along, you're forced to outwork your competition, thus enabling to you achieve that long-awaited dream. People often forget this when analyzing the data on whether one will succeed or not. – **CHAP-TER 5**

Like I said before, to achieve your dreams, you need someone to help condition you; you need someone to help bring you along. – **CHAPTER 5**

In the most meaningful relationships, each party must be humble enough to accept help from the other party. Without this, the type of learning and improved that is needed to become excellent can never happen. – **CHAPTER 6**

When you think outside the box, it not only levels the playing field for you and your competitors, it might even give you an edge to beat

146

them. Because your competition has more talent than you to begin with, they've never been forced to think outside the box; they've never been forced to be creative. If you remember this, you might just become like David and beat Goliath. –
CHAPTER 7

As an underdog, if you already know what the person who is highly favored is going to do, use that to your advantage. As the cliché says, "knowledge is power." If you already know what their move is going to be, you have the power then to make your move. Battle is like chess; it's how you respond and react; can you be bold enough to make the right move? – **CHAPTER 7**

We must get outside of ourselves if we ever want to make anything of ourselves. When we look deeper into what I just said, we can discover the reason for this. A synonym for outside is exterior. When we think of the exterior of a peanut butter sandwich that is given to a child, he/she often doesn't want to eat the crust, but our parents growing up demanded that we finish our plate. One of the ten commandments from Exodus is "Honor your father and your mother, that your days may be long upon the land which the Lord your God is giving you." Ultimately, Jamal honors his mother and himself by go to the new school. When we honor our parents and "finish our plate," we can start to get outside and challenge ourselves more and more each and every day. – **CHAPTER 7**

For any leader to be successful, you have to not only have energy, but provide it to others in abundance. One way to do that, believe it or not, is to deflect attention and praise away from yourself. This, in turn, puts the emphasis back on the people, challenging them to do the impossible. – **CHAPTER 7**

To get back on your feet after calamity has struck is not easy. But remember, with daringness comes determination, and with determination comes the possibility of the pursuit of excellence. With unthinking sureness, what was once a possibility can become fulfilled. But this can only happen if you take the chance to begin with. – **CHAPTER 8**

Marriage is a *big* deal to God—being in a dating relationship or being engaged, not so much. Never find yourself saying to yourself, "well, if I had only been single, I might have ended up with that right person God had in store for me." – **CHAPTER 8**

When people feel threatened, they attack, knowing full well that is the only way to get out of their inferior position. If you're conditioned correctly, there's always a way out, even if that means attempting the unthinkable and getting a little help on the way from friends. – **CHAPTER 9**

To get out of trouble yourself, you have to be conditioned to be humble enough to ask for help and realize that you can't do everything on your own. – **CHAPTER 9**

When you're the underdog, you're only used to this because you're conditioned to have everyone doubt you all along. This itself can be advantageous and can cause the lowly to triumph over the mighty. – **CHAPTER 9**

From The Pages of *Input-Output: Our Final Product Comes from Our Initial Actions*

These people have become my guide on how to live life. When you have a solid guide on how to live life, it impossible to fail. The guide will serve as not just instruction, but encouragement, too. If you find yourself making the same decision as the guide, your life will mirror their life. If you find yourself making the opposite decision, expect nothing but failure, for just as what lead them to their excellence will lead you to utter destruction. **– CHAPTER 1**

You see, when you hold yourself accountable for your actions, people on the other side will appreciate it. They'll appreciate your candor because if you can't pinpoint your own weakness, it is impossible to improve. **– CHAPTER 1**

When you seek out the advice of others, you enable yourself to draw on the intelligence of not just yourself, but other very capable people. The moment you deem yourself already qualified to make a decision alone is the moment you stop learning, thus resulting in an uneducated decision. **– CHAPTER 2**

So many times in life, there are moments of progression we miss that are just as monumental as marked success. If you can remember to pat yourself on the back when you accomplish these bits of success, you'll be well on your way to achieving goals. **– CHAPTER 2**

So many times people have opportunities to succeed without realizing it. **– CHAPTER 3**

We only have so much energy we can devote to certain things. Don't let your accomplishments become fewer because you're spending your energy on things you can't change. – **CHAPTER 3**

Adaption in circumstances requires not only flexibility, but a quick-thinking mind.   Those who can change in an instant last forever, while the obstinate cease to exist in all forms. – **CHAPTER 3**

When you inspire confidence in others, you have the ability to lift people higher than they ever imagined. In a sense, you give people wings to soar into the atmosphere with a continuous and permanent pace. – **CHAPTER 4**

Seeing potential in yourself is one way to have success, but as I said in chapter four, in order to have continuous success, you must trick yourself into normalizing your success for it to continue on. – **CHAPTER 5**

Never realize you're having success and you'll continue to have it. The moment you sense that you've "made it" is the moment you will slide into mediocrity. Keep pushing and know in your heart of hearts that you have "never arrived." – **CHAPTER 5**

The best aren't afraid of stress and often ask for more, relishing their innate ability to handle it, while the ones who sit on the side-lines will continue to sit there. An apathetic nature guarantees one thing in life for that person: because they strive for nothing, they get nowhere. – **CHAPTER 9**

You're going to face negativity from time to time if you ever attempt to do anything great. Rather than complain about it, harness it and use it as fodder to prove them wrong. When times are tough, try to imagine the look in your doubter's face when you do prove them wrong. One thing you can expect them to do, however, is admit that they were discouraging in the first place. **– CHAPTER 10**

Running away from the work that is required in the input is often times the reason why we don't see the output we anticipated. **– CHAPTER 11**

When at war, continue to play offense even when your enemy expects you to play defensive. It will catch them off-guard, and you will surely win. By continuing to play offense, it will tire them to the point where they can no longer compete, which will give you the opportunity to be victorious. **– CHAPTER 11**

The initial will always produce finality. **– CHAPTER 11**

Made in the USA
Monee, IL
07 July 2026

56546640R00085